Everything IS SUBJECT TO CHANGE

A Novel by

Greg S. Reid

Prindle House _ Sherpa Press

Everything Is Subject to Change by Greg S. Reid
Copyright © 2010 by Greg S. Reid

Prindle House Publishing Company
P.O. Box 18761
Jacksonville, FL 32229
www.prindlehouse.com

ISBN 978-0-9819372-7-4

Sherpa Press
8272 Gilman Drive #30
La Jolla, CA 92037
www.sherpapress.com

ISBN 978-0-9829850-0-7
Library of Congress Cataloging Data

Most great people have attained their greatest success just one step beyond their greatest failure.

—Napoleon Hill
Think and Grow Rich:
THREE FEET FROM GOLD

Appreciation

In addition to Scott Hove, Allyn Palacio, Greg Tobin, Twyla Prindle, and Don Green, special thanks and acknowledgment go out to all the leaders and dreamers who make this world a better place. They are always of service!

Introduction

Over the centuries, it is the author's and publisher's observation that lessons have best been learned through parables and stories passed along from one generation to the next. This book continues that tradition with a modern-day tale that reinforces the strategies for personal and business success that have stood the test of time.

Throughout these pages, you will be reminded of age-old wisdoms, which may rekindle the entrepreneur spirit that made this nation so great and that lies within you, ready to be shared with the world.

Enjoy—and whatever you do…Keep smiling! ☺

Contents

Life IS TREMENDOUS

FROM the look of the crowd filling their carts and lining up at the cash registers, it was apparent that the end of the weekend had arrived. Another Sunday afternoon, and the shoppers were out in droves. Erickson's, the local grocery store, was traditionally where the townsfolk gathered, swapped stories, caught up on local news, and shopped for the upcoming week.

A clean, well-maintained store, it had been family-owned for three generations, and the Ericksons still kept a close eye on the business that had carried their name for more than 50 years.

Tammy Conley, as her badge proudly proclaimed, was something of an anomaly at Erickson's and in this small California town where everyone knew everyone else's business. The single mother of two had dreams for herself and her children but kept those dreams to herself. Because in the past, when she had shared her aspirations, she had clearly sensed that most people would rather not hear about it. For as long as she could remember, she had secretly envisioned running her own clothing business, designing and selling fashionable clothes . . But rarely had she mentioned this aspiration to anyone.

Perhaps that's just the way it is in a small town. Other folks may sincerely care for you, but they also seem to want to keep you on the same track along with them, not ahead, nor behind. They're uncomfortable with ambition. Not that they don't want you to succeed—they just don't want to lose you.

So 31-year-old Tammy Conley, a trim redhead with hazel eyes and a nose that turned up prettily and attracted the attention of males in the store and elsewhere, did her job to the best of her ability. And she enjoyed it.

Always effervescent, Tammy invariably greeted her customers with a friendly, "Hello," and ended the sale with her patented catch-phrase, "Keep smiling!" Her own smile was permanent and real, and she carried it with her wherever she went, rain or shine.

The people shopping at Erickson's were willing to wait in Tammy's line, even if it took a little longer than others, just so they could enjoy her send-off for the day. Her flaming hair and bright eyes had become familiar to all who passed through Erickson's aisles for the past several years.

"Keep smiling," she beamed at another group of customers checking out their weekly groceries.

"Thanks, Tammy, we will!" The patrons left, seemingly grateful for the emotional boost.

She could not know it, but this day, August 4, would change Tammy's life forever. She concentrated on doing a good job with each individual who came to her checkout station.

"Hello, Mrs. Walsh!" Tammy greeted one of her regular clients. "How did the past week treat you?"

"Very well, my dear," the older woman replied as she held up her purse, ready to pull out the cash for her purchase.

"Did you find everything OK?"

"I found everything in here but a good man," the woman whispered as she leaned in to share her not-so-secret thought with a silent wink. Emma Walsh wore her steel-gray hair stylishly clipped and fashionable glasses.

The two had kept up the same routine for longer than either could remember, at least a couple of years.

Tammy thought about this successful woman whom the locals called "Wealthy Walsh." She had made her fortune by launching a business called TeleWorkout that she had then franchised and grown to over 200 branches across the globe.

It was a novel idea, a solid marketing concept that she ran with as far as she could—much farther than anyone would have predicted. How had it happened? Like most people, Emma Walsh had wanted to improve her own health, but working out in a gym wasn't an option. Not only did she lack the time, she simply wasn't willing to hang out with others who intimidated her as she did her best to improve her physique.

"Who wants to go to a club with a bunch of 20-year-old hard bodies that make me feel even worse about the way I look?" she would say. So, she had decided to look at her own problem as an opportunity and started TeleWorkout.

Her business model was simple and brilliant at the same time: Customers paid a monthly fee to join to work out in the comfort of their own home. They simply dialed a central conference-call number, put the phone on the speaker mode, and listened in with hundreds or even thousands of others at the same time as a physical trainer led the session.

What an idea! No travel, no gym, no pressure, no headaches—yet, you still got the same results as being in class down the street, and for many, the best part was not having to worry what others thought as you worked out in the privacy of your own home wearing whatever pleased you—even those tattered gym shorts you've held onto since high school.

"May I ask you a question, Mrs. Walsh?" the checkout clerk said.

"Of course," Emma answered. "What's on your mind?"

"I've been watching you come through these doors for years now, yet I never asked you how you became so successful. I mean, I know *what* you did, but the question is, *how* did you do it?"

"Great question, Tammy," the entrepreneur said in tone that was congratulatory. "I was wondering how long it would take until you got around to asking me that. The truth is I've wanted to share my little formula for success with you for the longest time."

"Why haven't you?" Tammy inquired.

"Because you never asked!" Mrs. Walsh responded. "You see, everyone *says* they want to be happy, healthy, and wealthy—yet so few actually achieve that balance."

"Why is that? Is it difficult?"

"Heavens, no. Actually, the formula is very simple."

"Can you teach me this formula?" the clerk inquired as she scanned another item in slow motion in order to keep her client there a bit longer to pick her brain.

"Of course, but before I do, you must do something first."

"Anything!" popped out of Tammy's mouth as if she were a contestant on a game show.

"Very well then, I will meet with you this coming Tuesday at noon, for coffee next door, but before you come I want you to read a book called *Life is Tremendous* by Charlie 'Tremendous' Jones."

"Consider it done," Tammy said as she packed the final grocery item into the recycled woven bag Mrs. Walsh always brought with her.

"Why that book, by the way?" the younger woman asked.

"Because you are about to make a change. In order to achieve a different result, you must first 'do' something different. The first step in my success formula is to begin reading great books and meeting new people."

Emma Walsh continued her thought. "Let me ask you, do you think your chances of achieving something that you desire would increase by associating with people who were already successful doing it?"

"Yes, of course," Tammy responded.

"Do you think your chances of succeeding would increase if you read less gossip from the checkout periodicals and read more positive stories about struggle and victory?"

"Sure."

"Well, there you go! That's the first lesson brought to us from the book you are about to read. Charlie says it this way, 'You are the same today as you will be in five years except for two things: The people you meet and the books you read. Hang around thinkers, and you'll be a better thinker. Hang around winners, and you'll be a better winner. Hang around a bunch of thumb-sucking, complaining, griping bone heads, and you'll become a better thumb-sucking, complaining bone-head."

Restraining her laughter, the wealthy woman continued:

"There are a bunch of people out there, many in this community and ones just like it across the country, who will make you think that if you read motivational books or hang around positive people you are doing the wrong thing. They may call you a dreamer or an idealist. The reason they act like this may be that deep down they know for themselves that if they want something more in life, they will have to make sacrifices and changes that they simply aren't willing to do."

Tammy said nothing as she absorbed the message, thinking to herself that maybe she wasn't so crazy after all for wanting more from this world. She also understood that something special was happening in this conversation. She was all ears.

Continuing, Mrs. Walsh pointed to the tabloid newspaper and magazine rack and said, "Unfortunately, many folks are interested in other's lives, and may even place more attention on some celebrity scandal than they focus on their own interests. You, my dear, are obviously different, and I look forward to sharing with you my little formula for success."

Although the mentor was offering Tammy the opportunity of a lifetime, her expression changed to a look of worry as she shared her concern is an ever-so sheepish tone of voice.

"I appreciate the offer to help me, I really do—only..." Tammy paused to compose her words. "I may not be the most qualified person to share your secrets with. So far, all I've known is setbacks and bad decisions. I mean, look at me: I'm 31 years old, still working as a cashier for gosh sakes. Two young kids. Single. No prospects, really. It seems like every time I've tried something new, to get out of this situation, I've botched it up miserably. I keep trying, yet here I am. Quite honestly, I often feel like a complete failure."

Emma Walsh looked at the young woman with warmth in her eyes and responded, "Well then, it sounds to me that you are the *perfect* candidate to help. Let me share something with you. Truth be told . . . *All my heroes are failures.*

"Fact is, everyone stumbles from time to time, and no great achievement was ever completed without its share of heartache and challenge. Every great leader had to fail *before* he or she could ever succeed. These are called 'life lessons.' The only difference with them is, they never let the mistakes dictate the final outcome, or stand in the way of their achievement."

Looking to her left and noticing she was the last one in line—a few other customers had given up and moved to other cashiers—Emma took the opportunity to share a wisdom nugget with her new pupil:

"I went to a seminar where the speaker, Genevieve Bos, said something that has stayed with me ever since. She said that the secret to success was, '*Never let your mistakes, setbacks, or circumstances determine your value as a person.*'

Noticing that the expression on Tammy's face had now become one of complete curiosity, she continued her point in dramatic fashion by pulling out a crisp $100 bill. She held it out, saying, "I saw this at another event one time, and am not sure who to give credit for it—yet you'll get the message." She then extended the money toward the cashier. "Do you want this?"

With an uncertain expression, Tammy answered, "Yes, of course."

Crumpling the bill, Mrs. Walsh held it out again. "How about now?" she asked.

Tammy simply nodded.

Dropping the money to the floor, Mrs. Walsh stepped on it. "What about now? Do you still want it?"

Not seeing where this was going, the younger woman said, "Of course—I'll take it."

"Why?"

"Because it's a hundred bucks, and I could really use that right now. It's the same $100 whether wrinkled or not."

"Then let me ask you something: Why is it, that when *we* get crumpled, thrown to the ground and stepped on, we think our value as a person changes? Our value hasn't diminished at all; it's just part of the process of what we're going through."

With a smile that could brighten the darkest night, Tammy immediately "got it." She enthusiastically exclaimed, "Thank you! That really makes sense."

"I thought you would understand," Walsh said in a friendly, intimate manner, tucking the $100 bill into Tammy's palm with a look of admiration and compassion.

A tear formed in the young woman's eye in appreciation for what had just happened—and what she hoped in her heart was about to unfold.

Reaching for her shopping bags and heading toward the exit, the stately woman offered a smile of gratitude, realizing that she had finally found that perfect person to whom she could pass along her knowledge. Tammy was someone who had discovered that she wanted to learn and appeared willing to do so.

Before she could reach the door, her new student called out: "Thank you, Mrs. Walsh. See you on Tuesday, and until then . . . *Keep smiling!*"

Tammy got home late, exhausted but jazzed in a way she hadn't felt for a very long time. Her life had been one of strict routine: Work, care for her kids, sleep, and more of the same the next day and the day after that—punctuated by a very occasional girls' night out with friends. She lived paycheck to paycheck, did not own a home, and had been virtually on her own since the divorce three years ago, with primary custody of David and Dana. There was always food on the table—even if it was mac and cheese much of the time. A lot of responsibility on one young woman's shoulders . . .

Because of the high cost of daycare, she depended on her mom to be with the kids most of the time when she was at work.

Tammy stepped into the house through the kitchen door and disengaged the alarm system. The TV was on in the family room. She could hear a news program and stepped into the dark room, illuminated only by the flickering screen. There, on the couch, was a sight that warmed her heart and made everything she had to endure every day worthwhile.

Her mother, Phyllis, sat there with Tammy's daughter Dana in one arm and her son David in the other. All three were sacked out, sound asleep.

At first, Tammy felt a pang of anger that her mom had not properly put the kids to bed. Then she quickly realized that there was absolutely no harm done, the kids were safe and sleeping. She would get them into their own beds soon enough.

First she whispered to Phyllis: "Mom. Mom. I'm home."

Her mother, at 59, had been a fulltime homemaker for as long as Tammy could remember. She had raised two girls, Tammy and her older sister Jane who now lived in New England with her husband and kids. Her husband, Tammy's dad, Jim, had died about 12 years earlier of a sudden heart attack. Tammy had still been a teenager, and she'd been close to her father—closer than to her mother, certainly—forever . . . That all seemed long ago.

"Mom," she repeated, touching Phyllis' shoulder and shaking her gently.

"Oh, hi, Tammy." Phyllis Conley awoke and rubbed her eyes, realizing what was happening. "The little ones fell asleep, and I didn't have the heart to wake them. I know I should have, but—"

"Don't worry about it," Tammy assured her. "Thanks for looking after them. How are you doing today?"

"Well . . . " Even in the half-light of the TV screen a shadow visibly passed over the older woman's face. "We have to talk."

In just a few minutes the two of them had gently moved both kids to their rooms and tucked them in. Phyllis and Tammy met up again in the kitchen. Tammy put on water to boil for tea. She and her mom sat at the kitchen table.

"Tammy, I have something to tell you. I can't put it off any longer."

"What's wrong, Mom. I know it is something. These last several weeks you haven't been yourself."

"I have breast cancer, Tammy. I spoke to the oncologist today. It's very serious. I'm going for surgery in three weeks."

"What? What do you mean?" The younger woman was having trouble processing what her mother had just said.

"It's pretty far along. I didn't know. There were no outward symptoms until I felt a lump last month. I had a mammogram almost a year ago and would be due for another pretty soon, but . . . it just came on real fast."

Tammy's eyes filled with tears, but she kept her voice steady. "We'll get through this together, Mom. You know we will. I don't want to lose you."

Phyllis grasped her daughter's hands in her own. The tea kettle whistled on the stove, but both ignored it. "I'm not going anywhere, Tammy. I'm here with you and the kids. Always."

Power OF MANY MINDS

As the door swung open and she stepped into the local coffee shop, Tammy felt a vibrant new energy. It was strange. Her mother's health crisis had stunned her utterly, but Phyllis had urged her not to let it stop her from moving forward. So, she had decided to follow her mom's advice and made an effort to be present at this meeting.

She breathed a quick prayer. Her genuine smile filled the room that was already redolent with the aroma of coffees and baked goods.

"Hello, young lady," Emma Walsh said as she came from around the table to give her a hug. "It's great to see you, but it is a shame you are on time."

"It's great to see you too! Thank you so much for meeting with me. This means more than you'll ever know." Then, as Tammy thought for a second, she said as they both took their seats, "Wait a second.

Why it is a shame I am *on time*? I thought that would be a good thing."

"Many of the lessons I will be sharing with you are based on observations and bottom-line facts I have learned along my journey," Mrs. Walsh explained.

"One of the common denominators I have found over the years is that great leaders always seem to be early for their appointments and meetings. The reason for this is that they are the creative brains behind most decisions and therefore are usually the most excited and engaged person in the group. On the other hand, those who show up on time, which you just did, are the managers of the world. They are the ones who clock in right on time, so they are put in charge of making sure everyone does the same. Now, there's nothing wrong with being a manager—but that isn't what you want, is it?"

"No, I want to be a leader. But what about people who are late?"

"Well, those people tend to be the employees of the workforce. They have little or no passion or interest in what they are doing, so it is not important to them to be anywhere."

"I have some friends who are late everywhere we go—and it drives me nuts," Tammy admitted.

"Chances are they have the employee mentality and no consideration of their employers. What is very interesting is that when it comes to one's personal life, it shows that they have little consideration for their friends, either—as their action proves."

"Wow, you weren't kidding. It does look like I need to get a new set of friends to get where I want to go. And, you were also right about the book by Mr. Jones. Boy, he does have tremendous insights. I couldn't put it down!"

"Where did you find the book?" asked the young woman's mentor, removing her glasses and looking directly into Tammy's eyes.

"It wasn't easy, but I found it in a small store way on the other side of town from where I live. I didn't want to order it online and wait even one day."

"That is an excellent demonstration of leadership."

"Of course, I am a leader. At least, I'm going to be," Tammy stated. "Now I understand why I have stayed the *manager* of the grocery store cashiers for six years. I should have been showing up early."

The wise woman laughed as she leaned forward to take a sip from her daily brew. "It seems you have the first trait of all successful people—and that's confidence."

"Confidence?"

"This single factor is the key to gaining and retaining true wealth. Those who believe they 'deserve' prosperity will attain it. Those who do not believe they deserve it, those who lack confidence, rarely, if ever, attain the prosperity they claim to desire."

Tammy said, "Is this why we hear so many stories of lottery winners who lose their fortunes in a year or two, or why sports stars sign huge contracts only to find themselves right back where they began financially? They took the actions to obtain the wealth, but they lacked the confidence that they truly deserved to keep it."

Mrs. Walsh said, "That may be the case. One of my favorite politicians, former Congressman Ed Foreman quotes something he learned from W. Clement Stone: 'Start saying positive, encouraging words to yourself, over and over until you begin to believe them: I'm happy, I'm healthy, I'm terrific.' Simple. Maybe it even sounds silly to you now. But it works."

Like a good student, the young woman sat there erect, listening, although Mrs. Walsh could sense some doubt or reluctance in her. A wisp of long red hair fell over Tammy's eye, and she pushed it back over her ear.

"You don't believe me do you, Tammy? Think of all the successful people you know, even your boss, and ask yourself whether or not they have confidence."

"Yes, a bit *too much* if you ask me," the student said with a shy grin.

"Of course they do! They believe in themselves, and therefore others believe in them too. Here's a challenge." The entrepreneur pulled out a yellow Post-It pad and slid it across the table. "Remember the other day when you said that some of the people around you make you feel a bit insecure when you talk about doing the things you need to do in order to make money, become confident, get ahead and be successful?

"Well, in order to counteract those negative messages, you need to take positive steps. So what I want you to do is write three positive statements in the first person. Then I want you to stick that note on the mirror in the bathroom or on the dashboard of your car where you have to see it each day. Every time you look at it, say those encouraging words to yourself. Better yet, say them out loud with conviction. The more you say them, the more you'll begin to feel they are true. The more you feel them in your heart, the more you'll believe them. And the more you believe them—the sooner they will become true!"

"Thank you. I'll do it now," Tammy replied as she wrote these words:

- *I am a leader!*
- *I am early!*
- *I am ready for a positive change!*

"I am ready for change. I—it's been a long time since I've said this out loud, but I feel comfortable here, with you. I want to create my own clothing line. I believe these words, and I believe in my own heart. Does that sound—?" She wanted to say "stupid" or "impossible." But neither word came out of her mouth.

"A line of clothing? It sounds very entrepreneurial to me. Remember, it's as simple as Benjamin Franklin said, 'God helps those who help themselves.' Tammy, that's why I am here now with you. First, you asked for assistance. That's why I am helping you. Then I gave you a task to accomplish by reading a book that has been so helpful to me. By taking action toward the recommended mission and showing up here today, you have accomplished something different than almost anyone else ever will ... you *did* something. And for that, I promise to keep working with you as long as you continue along this path."

"Thank you for that, and yes—I will continue," Tammy promised. "Is there anything I should do before we meet again?" she inquired.

"Let's plan to meet every other Tuesday right here at the same time," replied her mentor. "And your next assignment is to begin a 'mastermind group.'"

"What's that?"

"It is group of four or five like-minded people who share their thoughts, ideas, and positive energy with each other."

"Why do I need that?"

"Remember what Charlie Tremendous Jones says, Tammy: 'You are the same today as you will be in five years besides two things ...'"

"The people you meet and the books you read."

"Now that you have begun reading great books, I suggest you continue while starting your own network of masterminds." Emma went on to explain, "Now that you are serious about starting a business, you need to surround yourself with people who have done and aspire to do what you are trying to do."

"I could really use that kind of a group. I love the concept, but I already know nearly everyone in town, and there aren't too many people I would think meet these criteria," Tammy lamented.

"Look, this is a no-excuse zone. You either create success, or you create excuses, but you can't create both. Don't tell me what you cannot do. Tell me what you *can* do."

After considering for a moment, Tammy said, "I could run an ad in the newspaper and online and say that I'm forming a women's 'winner's circle' and am seeking others who want to encourage and support each other."

"There you go. Now you're thinking."

"Is there a reason for this, other than the fact it will be nice to meet new people?" Tammy asked.

"Absolutely. There are others who will tell us what we cannot do, where we cannot go, what we should or shouldn't say. So, wouldn't it be great to have a group of positive, solution-focused people helping you share in your dream and offering guidance along the way?"

"Yes, it would!"

"The mastermind group should meet once a month. Each member will bring a goal. At the meeting, share your goals with one another and then come up with action steps to make it happen. The strength of the mastermind idea is that the others will see and think of things that you haven't."

"I don't know yet what my goal *is*," adds Tammy.

"That's fine—we'll go over that the next time we meet," Mrs. Walsh answered. "Just get the ball rolling, and that's enough for now. See you in two weeks." She hugged her bright-eyed protégé good-bye.

Rarely had Tammy Conley felt so personally empowered. She remembered how she had felt on her wedding day more than ten years ago: On top of the world, with so many possibilities laid out in front of her, as well as her husband—whom she loved. The future had looked so bright and shining. So, what had happened…?

She sat down at the table in the coffee shop and picked up her cell phone. She called her mother.

"Hello?"

"Hi, Mom. Just checking in on you."

"That's sweet of you, Tammy, but you don't have to keep tabs on me every minute. I'm not going anywhere."

"I know, but—" She stopped herself. She didn't want to say out loud what she was thinking: But you won't be around very much longer.

For the tenth time that day, she said a silent prayer, asking for help from her God—not only for her kids and her mother, but for everyone in her life and especially for those who most needed his healing touch.

"Look, you're working a late shift tonight, so grab something to eat and get to work on time."

"Early," Tammy said, as much to herself as to her mom.

"What?" Phyllis said.

"Thanks, Mom. You've done so much for me all my life . . . "

"Don't be silly, Tammy. You've always given me great joy. I'm grateful you're my daughter."

Stop AND GO HOME

Tammy's head raced with what her new mentor, Emma Walsh, had begun to teach her. But her mom's situation, which first had come as such a shock to her, still gnawed at her spirit. What could she do to help her mother get better? Not knowing was the tough part, especially for Phyllis. And she knew it would be for Dana and David one day—all too soon.

Thoughts of her mom weighed on her mind as she worked her shift at Erickson's . . . And each time she rang up a sale on the register she was able to read the little yellow Post-It note with the affirmations she had written earlier:

- *I am a leader!*
- *I am early!*
- *I am ready for a positive change!*

She read the affirmations over and over again. As she did, she began to believe that her life was changing right before her eyes.

The best part, she said to herself, is that this change in the way I think is *my* decision and not due to the actions of another person or circumstance. She felt that she was in the process of becoming a new person as the direct result of her own actions, and she vowed to continue making positive choices from this point forward.

Tammy even began seeing each customer as a new prospect for her mastermind group, looking at them from a new light and direction while asking herself, "Is this someone I could learn from and support in return?"

The overwhelming answer to her question was a resounding "No." It seemed as though all her customers, whom she had come to know as acquaintances and friends over the years, were living the life that she was attempting to leave behind. She was ready to do whatever was necessary to break the chain of the daily grind in order to claim a new life that previously had only been a dream.

"Hello, girlfriend," said a friendly voice.

Tammy looked up to see a familiar face. It was Julie Browne, a 30-something woman who always stood out in a crowd. Julie was the type of woman everyone wanted to be like: She wore the nicest clothes, drove the nicest cars, and yet was the most humble person you could ever meet. Julie, however, had been a missing part of this small hometown feel for years.

"Wow, is it great to see you!" Tammy exclaimed. "Where have you been hiding?"

"As the old saying goes, I needed to go find myself," her long-time friend replied. "Now I'm back to see my family and, of course, I just had to come see my old friends—and you were first on the list!"

"So now I'm old am I?" Tammy asked teasingly.

Julie laughed. "So, tell me Tammy, what's new in your life?"

"You are not going to believe this, but Emma Walsh is now mentoring me. I decided I want to do something more with my life, and most important, I *need* to do it for myself and for my kids, because I've realized that no one can do it for me."

"Did she tell you to begin by reading books?" asked the long-lost friend.

"Well, yes. I began with *Life Is Tremendous* and just picked up another one called *Fish!* It's about how to have fun at work." Tammy stopped in her tracks. "Hey, wait a minute. How did you know that?"

"She did the same for me," Julie said. "You are in *very* good hands. In fact, that is why I ended up leaving here for such a long time. She taught me the most incredible lessons, and I needed to go pursue them. Because I took that action, I am now living my dream. I realized that the old cliché was true, 'If we always do what we've always done, we'll always have what we have right now.' And just like you—I wanted something more!"

"That's great to hear," the clerk congratulated, even while noticing that a line was beginning to form at her checkout station. "Can we get together and

STOP AND GO HOME

compare notes? I would love to find out what she shared with you."

"Normally, Tammy, the answer would be a resounding 'yes,' yet, considering that you are working with her yourself, I believe it's best for you to get it directly from the source. You are in great hands and I cannot wait to compare notes once you find your *knowing*."

"My what?" asked Tammy.

"You'll see, "Julie said reassuringly. "I am so excited for you, and I really do look forward to connecting again soon. Here is my cell number."

Julie handed Tammy an embossed business card. It was beautifully simple and understated, with only her name and number. The simplicity of it made an immediate impression on Tammy.

"Stay in touch, Tammy!" Julie said as she turned to leave the store.

"Wait, before you go, can you tell me just one thing to expect from meeting with Mrs. Walsh?"

"Well, OK. I'll share one quick story."

Tammy said, "That's great! I'm scheduled for a break right now and what better way to spend it than with a story from another of her protégés."

Taking a seat in the lunch room, Julie began: "There was a single woman who had a little girl named Heather, a blonde-haired, blue-eyed exuberant child who pushed her limits. Because part of a mother's job is to protect her children from injury and danger, boundaries were set.

"When Heather turned five, she wanted to ride her bike out of the driveway. They lived in a small subdivision with no sidewalks, and her mom wanted to be able to see her at all times. She told her she could go as far as the stop sign, which was two houses away. The rule was simple: When Heather saw the stop sign, she would 'stop and go home.' The rule worked great! Heather always turned around at the stop sign and came back home.

"About two years later, the woman was remarried to a great guy, and they decided to take their first family vacation to Disneyland. They were ready, with suitcases packed. They buckled the girl in and took off down the road. Less than a minute into their travels, they stopped at the intersection. Upon waiting for their turn to go, Heather said, 'Oh no,' and started crying. 'Now we must go home.'

"'What's wrong?' her mother asked.

"'You said we were going to Disneyland,' the girl cried. Heather pointed to the same stop sign she had always obeyed. 'There's the stop sign!'

"You see, it had been ingrained into her head that all stop signs really meant, 'Stop and go home.' Tammy, do you see the implications of this story?" Julie inquired, even as she began to explain.

"The word 'stop' means: *do not* progress, *do not* move forward, and, immediately discontinue the action at hand. When we were children, all kinds of 'stops' were given to us for our safety and well-being. Now we know, a stop sign simply means to pause, look for danger, and then proceed with caution. Now that we're grown up, many of us are still using the same old 'stops' of our childhood!

"How many of us are in our present circumstances based on things we were taught as kids? Some of those things might have been ingrained into our mind for a positive reason, such as safety. But now that we're mature, many of the old rules are still subconsciously holding us back. How often do people begin to get close to realizing their dreams, to changing their lives—and then they hit a 'stop?' Maybe they stop what they're doing because there isn't enough money to take the next step.

"Or maybe they stop because they are afraid to leave the safety and security of their current job because of the fear of the unknown. Tammy, you need to think about what will happen when you cross the boundaries, the 'stops' that have been ingrained into your thinking. Because when you get to that 'stop' you have two choices to make.

"The first choice is to do exactly what the sign says, 'Stop!' With that choice you will not move forward. You will not pass 'Go.' You will stay with the familiar and remain at status quo. The second choice is much more exciting; but you do need to decide if it's the decision you will make. Most people don't. With this choice, you follow that little nudge which gently pushes you to take the first step beyond your present boundaries. Then you discover that with each step, you are moving that much closer to achieving your goals and realizing your dreams!

"Two choices but with two very different results! Tammy, try to look at all the 'stops'—or whatever we call obstacles—in your life as positives. They are opportunities to push your limits, and find a way to move forward. They are momentary pauses on the path to success!"

Tammy sat quietly and finally responded, "That is one of the most profound things I have ever heard. As you were telling me the story and then explaining it, I realized how much I have to learn and how many things have been stopping me up until this point."

"My friend," Julie said, "you have done what so few people ever do. You have taken the first step by asking Mrs. Walsh to help you. I didn't make up that story. I heard it from her as she saw me doing many things that had been stopping me, too. I'm so excited for you! You have all it takes to reach all of your dreams and really live the life you love."

"I'm excited, too; but for now I need to get back to my checkout line because my break is over I can hardly wait to see you again, Julie!"

Amazing . . . Even as she applied herself to the most routine and mundane parts of her job, scanning and bagging items for her customers at Erickson's, she felt different—she *was* different, or at least becoming a different person. Could it be this simple? This profound?

"Keep smiling!" she told one of her departing customers, meaning every syllable with her whole mind, body, and spirit.

First THINGS FIRST

The week since Tammy last met with her adviser had gone by far more quickly than she could have imagined.

Now that her attitude and enthusiasm for life was at an all-time high, she felt she was well on her way along a positive path. At the same time, she realized, this new open road had always been there for her. She simply had chosen not to see it.

Her life had taken many turns—most of them unexpected. But, she knew, that is the very nature of life. Her "job" was to learn how to expect the unexpected and to understand that everything is subject to change. *Everything.*

Take her ex-husband, Tim Hartman, and their children, Dana and David. Dana was five-and-a-half, going on 15, and David was a wide-eyed four-year-old. Tim was thirty-five—also going on fifteen . . . or so it sometimes seemed to Tammy. She stopped herself from going down that path. She was determined to put aside all her resentments and past problems with him. She still loved him, though she was no longer *in* love with him. That was a big change she had only begun to come to grips with.

Lately, with her mom's illness, Tim had stepped up to the plate and taken the kids more often, which his parents, Tammy's ex-in-laws, really appreciated.

Tammy loved her kids beyond any calculation, more than life itself. And nothing—absolutely nothing—would ever come between her and those two little ones.

The story her friend Julie had shared with her about life's "stops" had also allowed her to see some of the barriers that existed in her life; yet, it had inspired her all the more! These insights, along with the upcoming meeting with Emma Walsh, made Tammy think, It's true that *when the student is ready, the teacher will appear.*

She reflected happily to herself, reaching for the door of the coffee shop. "Today is only my second meeting with my new mentor but it feels like I have already gained a lifetime of new information and a desire for learning."

Tammy found a seat and immediately began reading the latest book she had picked up at the local bookstore, *Think and Grow Rich: Three Feet From Gold* by Sharon L. Lechter, Greg S. Reid, and the Napoleon Hill Foundation. It taught people like her how to turn obstacles into opportunities. Little did she know that the message she was reading was right on track with what her mentor was about to share.

"There's my good-lookin' student!" exclaimed Mrs. Walsh as she entered the coffee shop with a bounce in her step. The woman seemed always to be a bundle of positive energy.

"Not only are you reading a good book, you are also early! Very nice!"

Tammy simply smiled in acknowledgment and laid down the best-selling book on the table.

"I have changed my mind," the mentor said suddenly. "I don't want to meet here every other week after all. I got a call from Julie, and she said you two spoke. She said she sees the same potential in you as I saw in her—so I have decided to show you something special."

The protégé's eyes filled with excitement as she asked, "Where are we going?"

"Just come with me!"

For Tammy it was yet another moment of decision. But it took no more than a split-second for her to choose what she would do. When she thought of her two children, what she wanted for them and for her own life, she followed her gut. It felt new, and it felt good.

The two got into Walsh's luxury sedan and drove away. Tammy had always loved the smell of a new car, especially one without crumbs in the back seat that her little ones usually left behind in hers.

As they traveled down one of the busy local highways, Tammy began to pepper her mentor with questions few people ask aloud.

"Why is it that most people never seem to do anything with their ideas? I mean, it seems that almost everyone has some great concepts and dreams; yet, so few actually do anything about it."

Without hesitating, Mrs. Walsh responded, "That's easy. You see, Tammy, one of the key ingredients for success can be summed up with one word. And, that one word is *focus*! While many people have heard the importance of placing their attention, they don't have a clue as to what to focus on. But, it turns out, that's the easiest part.

"What should I focus on?"

"The answer: *One thing at a time.*"

"You see, in this fast-paced, multi-tasking society, it seems we are judged by how many different things we can do all at one time. In reality, we can only do *one* thing *well* at any given time. I want you to imagine working with your computer. It has many capabilities and you decide to tap into almost all of them at the same time: playing music, checking email, working on a Word document, inputting numbers into an Excel spreadsheet, or improving a PowerPoint presentation."

"What do you think would happen to the computer? The system would move pretty slowly, right? The reason for this is that your computer also has limitations. When pressed too far with too many different tasks, it slows down and doesn't reach its full potential."

"Guess what? The same thing applies to us as human beings. We can do things faster and better, if we focus on *one thing at a time.* By trying to do too many things all at once, our own personal working 'system' slows way down, too!"

Tammy said, "These things you are teaching me are great. Everything seems so simple when you explain it. But I've got a lot going on right now. I'm juggling spending time with my mom, her health, providing for my kids, and now growing a business. When I'm at work, I try to focus, but I don't know where to start, and I get distracted easily. Then, when I have rare moments of down time—well, all those things flood my thinking all at once."

"I can help you with that," offered Walsh. "Let me ask you something—what would make you run through fire?"

With a head-jerk, Tammy turned toward her mentor, and in a skeptical tone she said, "Excuse me?"

"It's a simple question really. What would make you run through fire?" Mrs. Walsh asked again.

"Nothing, I suppose," the baffled student answered.

"Well, it sounds like that is your first quest: Once you know that answer, you can get on track to discovering your purpose."

"What do you mean exactly?"

"I have a good friend named Savannah Ross, who lives in beautiful Canada. She has become a great success in both her personal and professional life by helping people live lives of sustained abundance. People call her 'Rich Mom.' The way she puts it is this, she asks: If your home was in flames, would you run back inside to save your old gym shorts?"

"Absolutely not," Tammy said.

"What about your tennis racquet? "

"Again, no," replied the pupil, wondering where this discussion was leading.

"OK, now what if your children were in there, and they were crying for you to help, would you run in?"

Without hesitation, Tammy's demeanor changed. She sat tall in her seat, raised her head high, and said in a matter-of-fact way, "Of course, I would."

"Well, there you go. Before you told me that nothing would make you do it, yet when pressed, you found something that would. When Savannah shares this example, she insists that even ten firemen couldn't keep her away from that house. Life is like that on many fronts, even in business. Once you find *what would make you run through flames* in your career choice, nothing—and I mean nothing—will keep you away from pursuing it, with the same determination as saving your child."

"Has Savannah always been a success?" Tammy asked.

"Heavens no, she had more challenges than many of us will ever endure: from bankruptcy, being told her son was about to die, and a failing marriage, to literally having her house catching on fire. Yet through it all, she came out with a new perspective that has now influenced people like you and I across the globe. From her struggle, she found faith. From that faith, she found her passion, and with that passion she found freedom."

Tammy said nothing at first, as she took in the message, but she then smiled from ear to ear.

"The best thing I like about Savannah is that she is also a realist, claiming it wasn't until she quieted her mind to see the opportunities around her, that she took notice. As she says, it's hard to enjoy the view when skydiving—if you don't have a *parachute.*"

The two laughed aloud at the poignant observation. After two hours on the road, they entered the next closest city where the streets were alive from the international film festival happening for the entire week.

As the car came to a stop, Walsh turned to look Tammy dead in the eye and said, "Young lady, we have to find something that would make you run through fire."

"That's great advice. I'll start looking," Tammy said.

The two women get out of the car and blindingly bright camera lights began flashing. Tammy had never experienced anything like this before. In front of her was a red carpet that stretched all the way to the street as the valets greeted their arrival.

"Where are we?" asked the younger woman.

"This is what's called a celebrity gift suite," Emma Walsh answered. "This is where movie and television stars, as well as musicians and other celebrities come to collect their gift bags before the award shows."

"Oh, I've seen this on TV and in the magazines, but never thought I would be here in person. This is great!" exclaimed Tammy. "How did we get invited?"

"My friend Gavin Keilly owns the business," Mrs. Walsh explained. "It is the epitome of a 'win-

win' business, and that's why I wanted to show you around. You see, it's more than possible to make money, even a lot of it, ethically and morally—while doing something that would make you—"

"Run through flames." Tammy finished her adviser's point, smiling.

The mentor continued: "Many of the people who make others feel guilty about financial success have simply never confronted their own insecurities about wealth and find it easier to lay them on others."

The two walked through the draped doorway to see a "Who's Who" of the entertainment industry bustling around, collecting their free gifts and schmoozing among themselves.

"Is that—?"

"Yes, it is. Do you want to meet her?" asked the mentor.

"Do I ever!" replied the star-struck young woman.

As Mrs. Walsh introduced Tammy to one of her life-long idols, she received an autographed photograph, signed to her children. The expression on her face reflected the gratitude in her heart.

Tammy was sporting the widest, brightest grin of her lifetime. Even for her, this smile was huge—and no one had to encourage her to "keep smiling!"

The young woman who, a day earlier, had been passing grocery items across a scanner, was now sharing greetings with stars she had only previously seen on the big screen.

"This is fantastic! I cannot wait to give this to Dana and David when I get home. They'll flip."

Tammy and Emma walked around the suite for nearly two hours—meeting, greeting, and rubbing shoulders with America's brightest and best-known stars. On the ride home, Tammy questioned Mrs. Walsh even more, as if it were the Inquisition.

"How did your friend Gavin do that? How did he get all those celebrities to come? How do you make money giving things away? How did you . . . ?"

"Shush up and let me tell you."

Tammy became silent as the teacher humorously but firmly interrupted.

"It's very simple," she went on. "As I said, this is a true 'win-win' business proposition. It's a shame that more business is not done this way, because it can be."

As Tammy opened her mouth to ask yet another question, the look on her mentor's face was all she needed to hold back and make the gesture of zipping her lips and throwing away the key as Emma continued.

"Every business owner wants, or should want, celebrity endorsements for their products. Yet understand, this is very costly to hire someone as a spokesperson. A great alternative is to have a photograph of a Hollywood star using or holding your product. Because celebrities, like everyone else, love to get free gifts, Gavin came up with his own version of the celebrity gift suite concept and then made it happen. What a success it's been.

"Here's how it works: selected—and qualified—organizations pay Gavin's company a vendor fee to reserve a spot in a suite where they offer their product to the celebrities passing through. If the star accepts the item, he or she will usually agree take a picture with it. The vendor is then allowed to use that picture on their web site. As you might imagine, this is very helpful to their product credibility, since we live in a society obsessed with celebrities. When the hottest TV star holds up your new line of goods it adds value and panache."

Tammy sat in silence for another moment, nodding to let her mentor know she was paying attention. At the same time, she was absolutely amazed by what she heard about this business concept.

"When you break it down, it is such a great opportunity for everyone involved. The celebrity ends up with over $50,000-worth of free items. The vendors paid a small fee to be part of the event. Since there were nearly thirty vendors, the costs were dramatically reduced by being split among them instead of being absorbed by just one entity.

"Doing business this way everyone is happy and everyone is a winner. The celebrities receive gifts. The vendors get great celebrity photo endorsements. The volunteers who walk the celebrities around the room are happy because they get to spend the day with their heroes. And, bottom-line, a profit was made from hosting the program. So you can see how this is a true 'win–win' for all—and that's the *only* way to do business.

"Oh yes, one more thing. Being a philanthropist at heart, Gavin also gives a few free spots to charity, so that while the celebrity is leaving, if he chooses—which many do—he may donate part or all of the new gifts to the non-profit, where in turn they are able to auction them off and keep the revenue for their cause. It just doesn't get much better than this."

Tammy was mesmerized by what she was learning. Glancing down at the handful of autographs she would be presenting to her family and friends back home, she thought to herself how fortunate she was to have a woman like Mrs. Walsh mentoring her, and she recommitted herself to learning all she could about business and life.

Opinion VS. COUNSEL

Returning to her regular job at Erickson's Grocery wasn't as easy for her as it had been in the past. Tammy's mind raced with what she was learning, and as she went back to work, a number of things continued to move to the forefront of her thinking.

Tammy realized that her employer did not share Mrs. Walsh's "win–win" philosophy. Further, she was beginning to see more clearly that her fellow employees didn't share her attitude about their jobs—and about life in general. She realized that what she had sensed before was now evident: they had a negative disposition toward success. It was an unconscious choice, but it was a built-in mindset, nonetheless.

In fact, now that she was exposed to an ever-expanding new world of unlimited opportunities and positive people, her own standards had begun to rise.

She could feel herself becoming more empowered each day.

She concluded that she had been suffering the "Second Banana Syndrome." That is where one feels more comfortable being second-in-command rather than taking the helm and guiding the ship out to sea. It is a safe course to take, since one receives the benefits of being a manager without suffering the stresses and turmoil of being the actual boss.

With these realizations, Tammy had dramatically shifted her perception. She decided that she would no longer settle for anything less than the best and would begin to surround herself with others who felt the same way about life.

At the end of her shift, Tammy headed straight for the local newspaper office and purchased an ad to run in the personals section. Unlike the other ads in the section—such as those looking for a weekend date—hers announced that she intended to form a "mastermind group."

It read, "Seeking other like-minded women for mutual encouragement as we work toward the fulfillment and vision of our dreams! Must be able to meet weekly for a minimum of six months."

Julie Browne had taught Tammy that a successful mastermind group required certain ingredients for it to work. Importantly, they needed a defined frequency of meetings and length of term as Tammy had written in her ad. Mastermind groups, Julie taught, must focus more on the commitment to action and the pursuit of successful outcomes than on feelings and emotions.

At each meeting, every participant would state her future goals along with an outlined plan of how she was going to make it happen. In successive meetings, the masterminds would share the actions taken in the previous week toward reaching their goals.

Potential members know upfront that three missed meetings mean they will be asked to leave the group. Additionally, if someone shows up to a meeting without working her plan, she too will be asked to leave the group. The reason for this is to make sure that those who were serious about their achievements would be surrounded by people who follow through on their intentions, too.

The same day that the ad was printed in the paper, Tammy's phone began ringing off the hook! She could not believe how many other women in her community were seeking a group like this.

Tammy called back everyone who responded to the ad and asked them to meet her at the same coffee shop where she had first met with Mrs. Walsh. Her plan for picking her mastermind members was based on what she learned from her mentors.

There was one simple rule: Whoever showed up early for their meeting was in the group, provided she indeed proved to be of like mind. After interviewing 13 potential members, the group was narrowed to a total of five women, including Tammy herself. They agreed to meet the following week in the conference room of the local library.

She also saw a way to help those not selected into the group. With each person's permission, she put them in touch with one another. Then they, too, could form their own group if they chose to do so. Her goal was to share the positive energy that she was feeling, almost as if she were planting seeds that might someday grow up as flowers in a garden.

One night when she was putting her kids to bed, Tammy looked each one directly in the eye. She had told them a little bit about her newfound knowledge and excitement about what might lie ahead for them as a family. But they were too young to understand fully the philosophy behind their mom's new goals and high level of energy.

"You know I love you," she said to David as she tucked him in, then to Dana as she tucked the girl into her bed, as well. She added, to each of them: "You are the light of my life. Because you burn so brightly, you show me the way. Keep shining. Good night."

Later, as she lay in her own bed with the lights out and the house quiet, she felt a tear in her eye—sadness, yes, about things that had gone wrong in her life and her marriage, but gratitude, too, about the gifts and graces that her God had given her—in abundance.

And she prayed for Phyllis, that God would protect her, heal her, and keep her with the ones who loved her...

For the first mastermind meeting, the library allowed Tammy to serve decaf coffee and tea, with cookies brought by one of the members. The agenda called for each member to introduce herself and state her main goal. Valerie Sheppard, LeAnne Williams, Maile Andrus-Price, and Tina Marie each shared her "qualifications" to be a member of this elite team: A deep desire to succeed and a willingness to do the work necessary to reach her goals—as well as the willingness to help others along the way.

Tammy, too, had a dream.   She announced her intention to launch her very own clothing company. What would set her clothing line apart from others is that it would make women feel empowered and sexy at the same time.

Blouses would be trimmed with inspirational words set into the fabric in a feminine way. One sleeve might say, *"Believe,"* and the other, *"Achieve."* Skirts would have symbols of peace and joy sewn into the bottom border. Tammy shared that one of her friends in town was a talented silk screen printer and believed she was onto something. The others in the mastermind group agreed.

Tammy stated that before the next mastermind meeting she would meet with the printer, investigate pricing, and come up with three designs. Valerie, LeAnne, Maile, and Tina Marie each also committed to an action step they would take toward their goal before they all met again.

Tammy knew she just had to meet with her mentor and tell her the good news.

"Have I got something exciting to share with you," Tammy said in a near-fever pitch.

"What's up, Tammy? How did your first mastermind meeting go?"

"That's what I wanted to share. You were so right. Meeting with these other women was just what I needed. It's so nice to talk about my ideas without people putting them down. I know that with this group, even when we have challenges, we will find solutions rather than excuses. It's terrific!"

"That's the difference between opinion and counsel," Emma Walsh replied.

"Yes, I read that in the last book I finished," Tammy said.

"Then you know that opinion is usually based on ignorance or the lack of knowledge. Counsel, on the other hand, is based on experience and wisdom."

Tammy smiled quietly because she knew exactly what her teacher was describing as she had learned about it from the book, *Three Feet From Gold* and the other wisdom literature she had been reading each night.

Continuing, Mrs. Walsh said, "When I wanted to launch TeleWorkout, I went to several people to share the idea. Most everyone laughed at me and said it would never work. When I asked why, they said it just wouldn't. That was their opinion. These people had never run a workout business before, so what did I expect? It was my fault for asking them.

"Then I decided to talk to experts in the field who were already successful and the response was completely opposite. These people started giving me counsel. They said that what I was about to do would be difficult, because it had never been done before. But they were quick to add that if I was going to follow through, then, I needed *first to do this, and then to do that.*

"In other words, they gave me their counsel on the 'dos and don'ts' of the industry that they had learned along the way. What a great help they were! I began my first mastermind group the following day. I wanted to surround myself with people who would encourage me—not those who would just rain on my parade."

At this moment in their relationship, for the first time, Tammy offered a bit of wisdom of her own, saying: "In his book, *The Courage to Succeed*, four-time Olympian Ruben Gonzalez says, 'You want to hang around people you have respect for, not people you have influence over.' That has stuck with me big time."

"That's fantastic!" Mrs. Walsh exclaimed. "What a great way to sum it up."

Filled with a renewed sense of confidence, Tammy added, "I feel so fortunate to have asked you for help. I cannot believe I have let this information slip through my check out line all this time. Did you have a mentor that helped get you going too?"

"Not a mentor, in the true sense of the word, like I am meeting with you. But I did have virtual mentors. People I have continued to learn from. Through biographies, business books, lectures, CDs, DVDs, etc. It's amazing what one can gain from someone else's life journey."

Pausing for a moment, Emma Walsh had a look on her face as though she was deep in thought. "Looking back, there are a few people that I met that really did leave a mark on me," she said.

Tammy asked, "Will you share a couple of examples?"

With a warm look of admiration, Emma Walsh said, "Let me tell you about Holly Eburne. Holly is a wonderful woman who has dedicated her time on this planet to help people 'love their life, regardless of their circumstances.' I really admire her because she is not one of those 'woo-woo' people who believe that success will simply fall into their lap by 'thinking about it.' Holly understands that to have prosperity, health—and even romance—there have to be action steps."

"Action steps?"

"Yes, of course. For example, you cannot have wealth without saving and investing, any more than you can't get a quality date if you don't bathe or keep up your physical appearance. Our actions reflect our results. Holly says that anyone can 'win the game of life' by following one simple action that most of society will miss."

"What's that?" Tammy asked with her usual inquisitive expression.

"Three words: 'Look For Good.'"

Tammy absorbed the words, as the adviser elaborated: "If more people will simply 'look for good,' rather than seek out negativity, their life will change accordingly."

"Do you think people really like, or look for negativity?"

"Let me throw that back at you. What are the local news stations, papers, internet usually focused on—good news or bad situations?"

There was no need for a response, since they both knew the answer.

Mrs. Walsh continued: "Here's what Holly suggests. When life throws you a curve ball, say to yourself and to the world, 'Thank you.' Whatever happens in your life, say, 'Thank you.' For it is *experience* that will make you who you are. Common sense will tell us that when we look for good in everyday experiences, we will begin to *see* the good, the same way that focusing on the negative will bring us more of that. What would you rather have, Tammy?"

"Good, naturally"

"I know, and it's why I like working with you. When Holly shared this with me, it opened my eyes dramatically. So perhaps you can pass it on and help others look for good in their own lives too."

"You can count on it. Who else made a positive impact?"

Emma seemed pleased that Tammy wanted even more information. She mentioned a name that was near and dear to her heart.

"Alex Szinegh. Alex has a fantastic story. I met him at a seminar once, where he was speaking. What I took away will stay with me for a lifetime.
As an immigrant, he had to create his own opportunities in life, and just like Holly suggests, he looked for good everywhere he could. It's amazing what we take for granted living in America. Alex and his family cherished such things—simple and good things. His life of perseverance could be made into a Hollywood film."

"Tell me about him."

"It's funny really, and why I laugh when I think of his story. The take-away message though is this: 'Right Script, Wrong Day.'

"When Alex came to America he was not accustomed to the holidays and rituals that most of us have grown up on. As luck would have it, his family arrived in the States on October 31st."

"Halloween," Tammy interjected.

"That's right. Alex didn't have a grasp of the English language. As he hit American soil, he was taught only a few words to celebrate the occasion: 'Trick or treat.' He and his brother had a blast collecting goodies that night. Only, no one told Alex that asking for treats is a custom only done on the night of October 31st. So the next day, on November 1st, Alex and his brother excitedly put on their hand-crafted costumes and knocked on doors for candy once again."

Tammy giggled at the image.

"Every time a door opened, he would sputter, 'Trick or treat.' As you can imagine, almost everyone told him to beat it. Many, however, didn't know what to do exactly, so they just gave him left-over candies. As he tells it, he loaded up a pillow case with treasure.

"Now here's the moral. Alex showed up with the *right script, but on the wrong day*. You see, he didn't understand English. He knew only those few words. So when people told him off or said negative things, he didn't understand—so it didn't bother him. He just kept going door-to-door saying the few words he knew.

"The way he tells it—no one can talk us out of our dream, if we choose not to understand what they are saying."

"What happened next?" Tammy asked.

"As life moved on, and he learned the language—things changed. Alex said, 'Once I could hear, I began buying into other people's expectations.' Makes you think huh?

"Later in life, after he decided he was finished with being told what he could and could not accomplish, he then decided to become an example of the voices he kept hearing from within. He listened to every self-help audio and read every book he could get his hands on. He consumed information as a daily diet of success. Now, he is living a life that most could only dream. All because of that moment when he showed up with the *right script on the wrong day.*"

She shared the story with her mom that evening over a light supper and tea. Phyllis' condition was up and down, but this had been a good day for her. Phyllis laughed at the mention of the little immigrant boy trick-or-treating on the day after…a poignant image that brought back a flood of memories.

"You used to love being a fairy princess at Halloween. Remember?"

"I certainly do," Tammy replied.

"You used to say that you could help others and make them better with the touch of your magic wand."

"I really believed it, too. Maybe I still do…" she admitted.

Change
IS IN THE AIR

Five months earlier, Tammy had launched Keep Smiling Fashions. Several things ran through her mind simultaneously this morning:

- I went into my supervisor's office at Erickson's Grocery and resigned so I could work on my business full time.
- My mastermind group and new friends have been a greater support than I could ever imagine!
- My clothing line has really been taking off.
- My kids are proud of me for going after my dream, and what a great example I'm setting for them as they watch me grow personally and as a business woman!
- It's all happening so fast, it's scary. Thank goodness I'm so busy, I don't have time to dwell on my fears.

People in the community noticed the difference in Tammy's life as well—her neighbors, other school parents, and fellow church members.

"It will be a shame to have you go," her manager had said when she finally resigned her position at Erickson's. "This place will not be the same without you. But I understand, and, frankly, I really admire what you are doing, Tammy. I wish I had your courage. By the way, can I get another one of those inspirational blouses you made last week? I want to send it to my aunt for her birthday."

"Thank you for understanding," Tammy had responded to her now ex-supervisor as she gave her a hug. "And, yes, I'll bring you another blouse when I turn in my smock this Friday."

That is how it went wherever she would go. Those who knew Tammy for her famous "keep smiling" attitude now came to know her as the creator and founder of Keep Smiling Fashions. Tammy realized that she was now living the life she was destined when she had run into her old friend, Julie Browne, and shared the good news.

"Hi, Julie. I did it! I finally did it! I gave my notice. My last day is this Friday. I can't believe it! Even though it's already been an uphill battle I'll figure it out."

Julie asked, "What have you run into?"

"For starters, now that I'm my own boss, I realize that I still *have* a boss. Me. More important, I am my only employee. It is so darned frustrating to realize I am doing everything alone."

"That is just great! You are totally getting it, sounds to me that all you now need is *synergy*. "

"OK, I'll bite—what are you talking about?" Tammy said.

Pulling out her cell phone, Julie held up a finger in a hold-that-thought expression as she placed a call.

"Mike Corradini and Sam Khorramian are international speakers and serial entrepreneurs who have mastered the art of synergy," she told Tammy. "Their ability to make $1 + 1 = 11$ is that of true masters who can position their students and partners to achieve massive success. Individually, both Mike and Sam have launched and grown a number of successful companies—from a clothing brand, such as you are interested in doing, to a lead generation company and most recently a national real estate investment firm."

The phone was ringing, then it was picked up. "Sam here," the voice on the other side said.

"Hi, Sam, this is Julie. Listen, I'm standing here with a dear friend of mine Tammy and wanted you to share with her what you and Mike, your business partner, refer to as—"

"Synergy ?" interrupted Sam from afar. "Hold on a second, let me see if I can get Mike on speaker."

A few seconds elapsed, then two voices chimed in: "Hi there, Mike here," and, "This is Sam, I'm still on too."

Tammy leaned into the outstretched phone in Julie's hand. "Hello, gents, I understand you two are involved with something called synergy."

Julie and Sam laughed in unison as Mike broke in. "Let me explain. Years ago, my partner Sam and I were building separate businesses. Each one was doing OK, but nothing special. It seems that the harder we worked individually, the less we got things done."

Sam interjected, "It's true. Let me ask you something, Tammy. I'm sure you've heard motivational words such as synergy, teamwork, etc. Yet it wasn't until we understood the science behind these principles that everything started happening."

"Science?" Tammy asked.

"Indeed," answered Mike. "You see once we discovered the power of change that works, it all made sense for us, and that's when things took off like a rocket."

"Synergy, I assume," Tammy said.

"Exactly!" Mike explained: "It's just the word for the process of *combining* three parts to make one whole. Together, it creates something many times stronger than any one of the singular items. That's what Sam and I did. Separate, we fell short, we were not very strong. Yet when we combined our talents and added another into the mix—we created magic."

"I think I get it," Tammy said as she pulled a notepad from her purse and began to write. "Once I combine my new product line idea with a great textile supplier, and perhaps ask my past employer over at Erickson's to promote them in their stores as well, my business may grow stronger without me doing much more."

"You are spot on," Sam commented. "Once we realize that we can all do great things by finding ways to combine forces, relationships, and opportunities—rather than always competing against one another—great things happen."

"Thanks, you two," Julie said as she pulled the phone back to her ear. "Sharing your insights with us is a great example of doing what you preach."

"Anything, anytime," the gentlemen responded in unison.

As they ended the call, Tammy looked at Julie straight on, reached out to grab hold of her arm, and said lovingly, "I appreciate you. I also appreciate the fact that you and Mrs. Walsh don't just walk around showing off your success. You truly are a class act."

Julie took Tammy's hand in her own and said, "Get ready, you are about to experience an interesting combination of your own." Then she asked: "Are you keeping up with your reading?"

"Yes, as matter of fact, I read a new one by a guy named David M. Corbin called *Illuminate*."

"What's it about?" Julie asked.

"The author basically points out that nowhere in personal development does it say that to have a positive mental attitude we must avoid looking at negative situations. He says, it's true we cannot fix every problem we face, yet we can't fix any of them until we face them. You should get a copy."

"I like that." Julie typed the book title into her mobile device for future reference. "I think we've all had a few struggles that we needed to illuminate"

"Help me out here,"Tammy said. "I feel like I'm the only one going through changes. Give me a little insight to one of your challenges so I know I'm not crazy."

"For me, it was about fear. Let's face it, most people are crippled by fear of one sort or another. Fear of success, fear of failure, either way—it's still fear. One day while I was sharing my challenge, Barbara Pitcock, a business associate and friend of mine, told me I needed to become a 'Fear Fighter."

"Sounds like you said *fire fighter*," interjected Tammy.

"In a way, it is. The way she puts it, the same way most people run out of a burning building, a fire man runs right in—or, like you told me last week, you would run in to save your children. Fear's only enemy is action. The moment you take action, even in the slightest form, the fear begins to leave as you start focusing on the task at hand."

"That makes sense for me, leaving my full-time job to pursue my dream became easier with each step I took to make it come to fruition."

"Exactly,"Julie responded. "Barbara suggested one simple act that has taken me from idea to reality on many fronts."

"What's that?"

"She recommended I create a vision board. You probably heard about that in the book and movie, *The Secret*, yet she takes it a bit deeper. Her suggestion is that we *see* ourselves in the pictures we place upon the wall. For example, I went and sat in the car I wanted and had someone take my picture in that car. With me at the wheel. Then another picture standing on the porch of the house I've always wanted. This way, I saw myself in the vision rather than someone else. When I couldn't be on the yacht or island I wanted, I placed my picture on the poster so I could be there in spirit."

"That's great. I love it! "

"By taking even the smallest of steps, it will trick your mind into believing the image more than your circumstance. She explained that the subconscious mind doesn't know what's real or imagined. So if you need more sales—envision it. Place a picture of what that looks like to you so you have to see it every day. Then pick up the phone and make one call. As ridiculous as that may seem, it's that action and imagination working together that will create magic."

"In my case, it seems that many times when I get started, something happens that derails me." Tammy said.

"Then get out of God's way," Julie replied. "Again, Barbara Pitcock points out that the main thing we can do to assist our success is to allow it to come to us. How many times have we asked or prayed for help, did the legwork to create the vision, and then allowed roadblocks to stand between us and that reality. If we truly believe that our higher power is there to assist us—then get out of the way and begin seeing and accepting the opportunities placed before our very eyes."

Opportunities...creativity...dreams...change. The messages were coming at her fast and furious. Amid the flood of inspiration and information, Tammy remembered another thought that held it all together: Everything is subject to change.

For good or ill, for better or worse. She thought of her mom in moments like this. Phyllis wouldn't be around forever. Everything is subject to change. This, too shall pass.

The ONCE I'S

Looking at the calendar once again, Tammy could hardly believe that it was May and that another few months had passed so quickly. Where does time go? She wondered silently, with a private smile. Where had her life gone, up until now? Perhaps more importantly, where would the next day, the next month, and the next year take her?

Her mom had stabilized somewhat, though she wasn't improving. The kids were getting restless as the summer approached, which is what kids do . . .

"This is going to be an unbelievable summer," Tammy thought to herself as she folded another set of her designs, placing them on display in the window of her new retail store.

Tammy had taken the advice of her mastermind group and opened a shop. She had also hired a web developer to get her online so she could both have a worldwide presence and drive customers to her brick-and-mortar location. Most importantly, she began associating with the top leaders in her field.

One of the best lessons Julie Browne had shared was, to be successful at anything, one should go hang out with others who are already doing what you want to do. Observe what they do, follow their lead, learn from their experiences, and add your own unique style. Julie had guaranteed Tammy that doing this would cut the learning curve for her by tenfold.

With this in mind, Tammy started going to every clothes boutique she could find and attended seminars and workshops about the retail clothing business in the current economy.

Tammy even attended the MAGIC show in Las Vegas where all the top vendors, manufacturers, and retailers meet each year to show off their new fashions for the coming year. It was like Disneyland for a designer! It was an expense that she first questioned and thought a lot about, then decided to invest her resources—and herself—in the trip.

Even though she didn't have a booth there, she tucked a few of her blouses into her purse and asked various successful designers for their input. This was her way of seeking "advice" and not just "opinion."

The input was unanimous and became a big part of the deciding factor in opening her store in the first place. She received compliment after compliment, based on her latest garments and slogans.

With a slogan suggested by her new close friend and mastermind partner, Valerie Sheppard, Tammy conceived an entire line of women's casual wear that she called, Happy to Be Me.

Just as Tammy would always say, "Keep smiling," Valerie understood the importance of being comfortable in your own skin in order to achieve a positive, optimistic, and empowered attitude for other women.

She had put it this way: "Many people in life seem to *feel* small in their own minds, when in fact everyone has something special to share. We live in a society that compares us to one another and creates envy and ill will. We need to catch ourselves and reflect about what is truly important. 'Gee, if I only had her husband, or that job, or their situation, then everything would be better,' just doesn't work anymore.

"We are all of the same essence," she had said more than once at their meetings, "and it's time we acknowledge the wonderment of who we are and gifts we have to share with others."

When others asked, "OK, I get that, now *how* do we do it?" Valerie would respond, "Notice what you notice"—meaning, when negative thoughts pop into one's mind, simply take one minute to stop and notice what you are experiencing at that moment. Does the stomach tighten or mind race, do negative images pop into your mind? It's time to replace those thoughts with a more powerful expression. How about this: 'I'm happy to be me!'"

Valerie expanded her point even further: "It's OK to want more financial freedom like Bill Gates or social connections like Oprah—yet at the end of the day, have appreciation for who you are. Work toward incorporating those characteristics into your activities, and add your own spin on it. Never let go of the beauty and wonderment of simply being yourself: Success, flaws and all. After all, as the saying goes, 'God doesn't make junk.'"

Valerie provided a tremendous lesson when it was her turn to share at a recent mastermind group. She handed each woman there a raw egg.

She said, "I want everyone to imagine being in the kitchen about to make some breakfast. The dog's barking, kids are screaming upstairs, and your husband needs to be out the door in 20 minutes. As you reach for the frying pan, you accidentally drop that egg, and it splatters all over the floor. What pops into your mind? Do you think, *Whoops?* Oh well, got to get another egg. Or does your self-talk sound a bit harsher? You are stupid! Look what you've done. Are you an idiot or something?"

Then placing the egg on the board table in a gentle fashion, Valerie said to the group, "Whatever that conversation going on is will be a direct reflection of how you see yourself. Here's the kicker, knowing this truth of who we are is the key that gives us the freedom to become the best *me* one can be."

One could hear a pin drop in that room. Point taken. Directly from that messaging, Tammy created the new line of outfits that remind anyone who wore them, "It's OK to be me. In fact, I'm happy to be me . . ."

"Hello!" called a potential customer as he entered Tammy's store one afternoon early in May. He was a pleasant-looking man with short hair and neatly dressed.

"I noticed a woman wearing one of your blouses the other day, and she told me she bought it here. I want to get one for someone special to me," he said.

"Well, thank you for coming in," responded the store owner in her usual welcoming tone. Her time spent and the lessons learned at Erickson's Grocery had stayed with her. "Everything you see in here is embroidered with a positive message. Take your time and look around, and let me know if I can help you find her size."

"These styles are great!" exclaimed the customer. "What inspired you to make them?"

"We all need encouraging words in our lives. Since the newspaper and TV are loaded with less than positive messages, I decided to take matters into my own hands and create something that would constantly remind us how special we all really are. My clothes are personal, positive billboards!"

"Did you just think this up?"

"Actually, no. They came from an idea I had years ago, but simply put off doing anything about it. I was afraid that someone would steal the idea if I shared it, or that nobody would buy them if I made them. You know how it is," Tammy replied honestly.

"What made you do it now?"

"I had to get over my stumbling blocks. Like others, I had my own great ideas, dreams, and desires. Yet I didn't follow through. I was always waiting for the perfect time. I convinced myself, I'd get started:

- *Once I* found that perfect job.
- *Once I* got some money saved up.
- *Once I* found the right people to back me.

- *Once* I've raised the kids

"You know how it goes. But what I didn't see is that there is *always* a perfect time to get started, and that time is *now*! So I just did it"

The customer stepped back as Tammy raised her voice almost to a shout, with maximum enthusiasm and confidence coming through in her body language, as well.

"By the way, my name is Bill Frase," announced the kind man as he reached out to shake her hand. "I love that enthusiasm. And love the way you described that. I've always called it a 'But Freeze.'"

Now it was Tammy's turn to ask him to repeat himself.

"A 'But Freeze,'" he said again with a smile. "Just as you explained a bad case of the 'Once I's,' here's another way to look at it. Back in school, we are all trained that when faced with fear we have two reactions."

"Fight or flight," Tammy interjected.

"Exactly. There is another form of fear that few actually acknowledge. The deer-in-the-headlight scenario. We've all seen examples of animals freezing when they think they're in danger. Well, people do the same thing without even knowing it. Every single day I see people stopped cold by this unconscious pattern. Once we're aware of it, we can break this automatic reaction when we know what to look for."

He went on, "So, whenever you think or hear the word 'but,' chances are you are in the middle of a But Freeze."

"I've heard of a brain freeze, but never one of those," the shopkeeper said, interested to hear more as her customer continued.

"There you go, great example. Anyone who has eaten too much ice cream too quickly has experienced a brain freeze. In a brain freeze, you stop eating the ice cream until the pain goes away, then you continue eating more slowly.

"A But Freeze has a similar reaction to a brain freeze. It makes us stop what we're doing, especially when it brings up feelings of fear. For most of us, our brains are wired so that signals are sent to our body to prepare for danger as soon as the possibility of change looms.

"Your brain and your entire being like certainty and familiarity. When we are in pursuit of something outside our comfort zone, the brain is sent strong messages that we want things to change in a big way. This puts our unconscious into survival mode without even knowing it. People don't like the physical sensations their brains are causing, so they stop immediately. They freeze like a frightened animal would.

"They usually have no idea why they have stopped taking action toward their dreams. They will usually buy into the excuse they thought or said after the 'but.' They don't stop because the excuse is actually true. The excuse allows their mind to think that there is a good reason for not going after what they really want."

"What a great message," the businesswoman said. "Would you mind if I put that quote on the back of some shorts? Some of my customers might get a kick out of the 'But Freeze' message plastered on their backsides."

"Absolutely!" Bill Frase agreed. "That would be great. And let me have these three skirts." He handed them to Tammy's sales clerk while finishing his thought. "Remember this—paying attention to every 'but' you think or say is the key to recognizing when you are freezing out of fear instead of taking appropriate actions that will get you closer to your goals."

"I totally get where you are coming from," Tammy said. "When the light bulb went off for me, that *I* was the one holding me back—not everyone else—it was all the inspiration I needed to stop saying what I *should* do and actually go do it."

Before they could continue their conversation, another patron walked in.

"Greetings, my dear!" Julie Browne said as she stepped inside with a look of pride on her face. "You did a great job in here! It looks like you are bringing some style to our little town."

As Tammy gave her a hug, she introduced Julie to Bill Frase as her personal co-mentor.

"Glad to meet you," responded the shopper, getting far more than he expected when he began his purchase. "Tammy, thank you for the clothes and for the motivational story. You've really got something special here." He grabbed his bundled items and headed out the door of the clothing shop.

Turning to her friend, Tammy said, "Julie, how are you? It's great to see you!"

Julie responded, "I just wanted to visit and see how the store is doing. Let's meet up next week."

The two agreed to meet for coffee the following week. Tammy had more questions in her mind, and she had some long hours of work and planning ahead.

Phyllis Conley's condition had rapidly deteriorated over the past two weeks. After consulting with her mom's doctor, Tammy reached out to a local hospice service to find out what the options would be if Phyllis did not rebound but kept going downhill.

She did not share this with her mother. Not yet. There was still time, she hoped and prayed. Outside, the sun shone longer each day, and wildflowers seemed even wilder and more numerous this year. Why was that? she wondered.

All ABOARD

The phone always seemed to ring at the strangest times. Just when Tammy was thinking that she had not heard from Emma Walsh for a while, there she was, calling to check on her pupil.

"Hi, Emma. It's nice you called today. Well, it always is."

"Young lady, I have a little surprise for you," Mrs. Walsh said excitedly.

"What?" Tammy asked, her curiosity piqued.

"You'll see. I want you to meet me at the Morena Del Ray Boat landing next Sunday at noon. Can you make it?"

"Absolutely!"

"Great, see you there and be sure to bring a stack of business cards with you."

Three months along, Phyllis Conley was having difficulties with her chemotherapy regime. Not only was she incredibly weak, but the powerful drugs made her nauseous and cranky. Tammy visited her every day, sometimes spending hours at her mom's house, helping with laundry and other chores, sometimes just sitting there chatting or reading to Phyllis from one of her inspirational books. These days, she always carried a book and a note pad, wherever she went—constantly feeding her thought process with positive motivational messages and information that she could apply to her business.

Phyllis asked about her grandkids: "How are they doing? I miss seeing their little faces as often as I used to."

"Well, they miss granny-sitting too," Tammy offered. It was true—and one of the most painful aspects of her mom's illness.

Of course, pre-school for David and Kindergarten for Dana kept the two little ones occupied during the day. And Tammy had become much more reliant on their other grandparents, Mary Beth and Felix Hartman, her former husband's folks.

They, in turn, were thrilled to have the kids more often. And they were supportive of Phyllis in her difficult illness—in quiet ways that Tammy's mom knew nothing about.

A week after Emma's call, Tammy stood at the end of a pier. This was no mere fishing dock, but a huge marina. The harbor upon which she gazed held some of the largest and expensive yachts that money could buy. She shielded her eyes from the bright sun to take in the sights. Her red hair appeared almost on fire in the sunlight.

Walking toward Tammy along the pier, Emma Walsh sported what looked like a feminine version of a sailor's suit, which fitted her well and made the most of the maritime ambiance.

"Cute outfit. So tell me, what's the plan?" Tammy said.

"We are going out to sea, of course," responded Mrs. Walsh in a matter-of-fact way. "Only we will be joined by two hundred quality ladies such as yourself, whom you'll be able to meet and network with."

"Wow! I didn't know that a thing like this existed," The younger woman said as they walked toward the waiting ship.

"That's because it's not open to the general public," Emma went on. "It's a private membership opportunity available to a select group of women run by a dear friend of mine, Desiree Doubrox. It's called 'An Empowered Woman.' As you will see, birds of a feather truly do flock together, especially if you know where to look. These ladies are of like mind and come together to share their experience, strength, and desire to help each other succeed in life."

Within seconds one could feel the energy of the gathering. Everyone was dressed to the nines. They hugged each other and shared the friendliest of greetings.

Taking in the energy around her, Tammy said to her companion, "I always thought it would be hard to find a group like this. To be honest, besides you, Julie, and my small mastermind group—almost every other woman friend I know seems more into herself than others. In fact, every time we girls from high school get together, it's like one of those scenes from a reality show you see on TV where everyone ends up bickering."

"That's a shame. It sounds like you are just where you need to be, then." The voice was that of a stranger standing next to her.

It seemed that Emma Walsh had left her side a few moments before, and Tammy was left standing there sharing her observation with a complete stranger.

Turning a bright shade of red, she offered an apology. "I am so sorry. I thought I was talking to someone else."

"No need for that." The woman's tone was friendly, just like Emma's. "Like I said, it sounds as if you are at the right place. Welcome. My name is Desiree Doubrox, and this is my group. Emma suggested I come over and introduce myself. "

"Goodness, I don't know where to start," Tammy replied, wanting to bombard the host with questions. "Where did you get all these people from? How do ladies join your group? When did all this begin?"

Before she could ask another, Mrs. Walsh stepped back in and took over the conversation. "As you can see, Desiree, I wasn't kidding about her enthusiasm level."

All three laughed aloud.

"I have to run and check on things before we go," Desiree said, "so make yourself at home. I'll answer all your questions as soon as I can. Emma suggested that we have a meeting with just the two of us at a later date. Enjoy yourself."

Turning to her protégé, Emma Walsh shared a story.

"I love what she is doing here with all these ladies. It reminds me of another friend I have in Chicago whom everyone simply calls Captain Ron. What a great guy. One of the nicest people you'll ever meet. Just like our friend Gavin with his celebrity suites business, Ron too looks for opportunities where everyone wins and can come away happy for being involved. What Ron Freeman does is similar to our adventure here, yet with a twist. As fate would have it, Ron's father has a wonderful yacht in Lake Michigan, yet cannot drive it alone due to its enormous size. Being a real estate investor, with many friends who can crew the boat, Captain Ron realized there is no better way to get people away from the ringing cell phones and fax machines than to get them off shore."

"What did he do?" Tammy asked.

"He created a perfect solution. Every month or so, weather permitting, he invites past and future clients out for a cruise. People love it, and the skyline from that perspective is second to none. His father is excited, because he gets to get out on his boat. The clients like it, because it's a stress free way to relax and meet new people. And Ron loves it, because he gets to drive and to gain new prospects. That's why they call him Captain Ron."

"Love it!" Tammy exclaimed. "And I love this boat too. What a great way to network."

"I knew you'd get a kick out of it. Wait until you hear the guest speaker."

"Tell me more about Ron."

"By trade, he's a real estate investor who focuses on joint venture opportunities."

"What does that mean?" asked the student.

"It's basically the same as Julie taught you about combinations, what some call 'synergy.' He brings his experience, connections, and insights to the table that would take decades to gain on your own. Although he works with seasoned professionals, his true passion is helping newer investors get into the business. What he does is literally take someone under his wing, and not only walk them through the process of finding a positive cash-flow property, he actually teams with them along the way, sharing in the profits and risks."

"Considering he's been doing it a while, I bet the risks are diminished because he knows what to look for and stay away from."

"Exactly," Walsh said with evident pride in her voice. "Now I want you to meet someone else. She is out on the deck—over there in the blue dress. Go up to her and let her know I sent you. Her name is Iris Hirsch."

As always, Tammy did exactly what her mentor suggested.

"Hi Iris, I'm Tammy Conley. Mrs. Walsh said we should meet."

"Hello there, young lady. Don't you look fantastic?" the woman said, admiring Tammy's colorful attire adorned with positive messages. "Emma is such a sweetheart, and she can't stop raving about you. It's a pleasure to finally meet you."

"That's nice of you to say," Tammy responded. "Here is my card. Please let me know if I may ever be of service to you."

"Well, look at that. A chip off the old block. I can see that she is teaching you well," Iris complimented. "She wanted me to share something with you about the importance of writing your own life story."

"What do you mean?" asks Tammy

"Have you ever noticed that sometimes other people want to thrust their thoughts, ideals, and expectations upon you more than they focus on their own existence?" offers the new friend. "It's the old 'do as I say, not as I do' sort of thing?"

"I teach that program to my kids all the time."

"Understood," Iris said. "It's important to teach that routine to children to keep them safe. Only as we grow older, it's imperative that we start gaining clarity toward what is important to us."

"How do we do that?' asks the guest

"We do that by staying anchored and not allowing our past negative experiences to color our current reality."

"Again?"

Taking Tammy by the arm in a gentle fashion, Iris Hirsch pulled her in and said, "It's so important to understand that we are the author of our own life. We can use our previous experiences to teach us, or hold us back. Fear can both motivate us, or make us run away. Fact is, life is filled with all kinds of unique moments that may be used to spring us forward or keep us frozen in our own tracks. My dad always said to use our LUCK: that is, Labor Used Correctly with Knowledge. This means, the harder we work, the luckier we get. So you see, Tammy, we get to determine what direction we wish to follow."

"How do you overcome the fear though?" Tammy inquired.

"That's easy. Ask yourself three simple questions: What's the worst thing that can come from this situation? What's the best thing that can come from it? What's the most likely thing to happen? What you will find is, people will see that the worst isn't so bad, the best would be wonderful, and considering hardly anything goes as planned, we're worried about the wrong thing anyway."

Tammy burst out laughing at the simple wisdom, while Iris continued her message.

"In other words, write your own story, be sure to keep an eraser handy, and whatever you do—be sure to color *outside* the lines."

"Love that, yet what about people who have had horrible things happen to them?" Tammy interjected.

"Great question," Iris replied. "We have all had horrible things happen to us. Nobody goes through life unscathed in a perfect 'Leave It to Beaver' world. The only difference is, how we use these experiences will determine our character. Meaning, character is not created by what happens to us but by how we handle the situation. Those key moments reveal who each of us is as a person and allows us to write our story by ending a new chapter in life."

Tammy did not speak at this point. She simply turned to her right so the two could stand shoulder to shoulder as she took in the message and the beautiful sights of the water, sky, and shoreline around her.

Before the two could resume the conversation, another passenger walked up and introduced herself.

"Hello ladies, I'm Roxane Marie. Emma suggested I come out and meet you two."

Tammy said: "For her to have sent you out here, chances are you have a terrific message. I don't want to put you on the spot, but could you share a bit about your background?"

"Yes—and yes."

It didn't take Tammy long to realize that this smiling woman was a bit different than the others. Her unabashed gentle spirit could be felt the moment she walked into a room. "Like I mentioned, my name is Roxane Marie Schwabe, and what I do for a living is also part of who I am as person. I like to introduce myself as an 'Inner Light Guide.'"

Both Tammy and Iris, were taken back by the description, yet equally intrigued.

"Let me explain," Roxane Marie continued. "Our lives are a reflection of the quality of the internal relationship within ourselves. We all have a powerful message within us that calls us to a higher purpose. I help people 'listen' to what that higher purpose is and grow their capacity to trust their intuition."

Tammy unfolded her arms and said, "What do you suppose keeps us from listening to that voice?"

"It varies from person to person, yet in general, we simply lack the experience or understanding of seeing ourselves as true creators. We're accustomed to using our physical and intellectual power to provide for and protect ourselves. Funny thing is, the more we succumb to the people and things around us, the further away we are from our inner voice. At some point in our lives, however, we wake up one day wanting more. More life, more love, more freedom. The secret is to free ourselves from that outside 'monkey mind' chatter we unconsciously buy into. Rather than keeping up with the Joneses, we can take an opportunity to listen to what we truly want out of life."

Enjoying the conversation, Iris said, "I love that term, monkey-mind chatter. I have always taught my clients to work on quieting the mind, because once we do, we can finally hear what we are attempting to tell ourselves."

"Hmm, how can I hone my intuitive abilities? I hadn't really thought about developing them to help my business," Tammy pondered aloud.

Roxane Marie answered, "Tammy, allow space for your personal growth to unfold in its own time. Review yourself gently and let go of the inner critic that judges you to be better or different. Listening to that critic simply zaps your creativity. Instead, learn to clear your mind of thoughts that sabotage your mission. This is just as important as clearing your desk and calendar throughout the week. Common sense tells us that the clearer things are, the easier it is to see what's important."

Iris and Tammy simultaneously turned toward one another and gave each other that "aha" expression as Roxane Marie finished her thought.

At this moment, Desiree came out on the deck and announced: "Ladies, we are about to set sail. You may want to grab a bite from the buffet before we take it down. Tammy, I really want to speak with you and have my hands full right now, so I will have my assistant get with you and set up a day for us to sit down soon. Are you all ready to go?"

As she told David and Dana about her day aboard the yacht, they listened to Tammy as if she were reciting a fairy tale.

"Mommy," Dana asked breathlessly, "can you tell us more about the lady in the sailor suit?"

"Good question, Dana," the girl's mother said. "Mrs. Walsh has become a very good friend and adviser to me. I call her my mentor. That means I ask her a lot of questions and listen carefully to what she tells me."

"You mean, like I ask you a lot of questions?"

"Yes, exactly," Tammy said.

"Then, she's like *your* mommy?"

"Well, no, I have a mommy. Your grandmother Phyllis."

"Do you ask her a lot of questions?"

Tammy swallowed hard. She looked at David whose eyes were heavy. He'd soon be zonked out. Then she looked into Dana's blue eyes—and there she saw herself. She remembered there had been a time when she had hung on her mom's skirt and asked her questions and bugged the heck out of her.

She said to her own daughter, "I used to ask. And, you know what, I'm going to ask her some more questions next time I see her. Tomorrow."

Rein IT IN

Tammy arrived at the coffee shop where she and Mrs. Walsh had met the first time—fifteen minutes before her. She ordered her coffee and sat down to go over her day's goals and objectives. Once that was done she began to read her current inspirational book.

"This is great!" Emma exclaimed as she walked in and saw Tammy. "I'm early and you are earlier! It's nice to see how many positive steps you've taken since we began our journey just a short time ago."

Tammy said, "It's become a new habit now. I'm always early—and I find I have more time. I'm teaching my kids the same thing."

"Which book are you reading now?"

"One that is helping me set my vision even higher. It's the original personal development book that started it all, *Think and Grow Rich* by Napoleon

Hill. You had recommended it awhile back, and now I see why!"

"Tammy, I'm so proud of you! You are doing all the right things. Keep filling your mind with positive things such as those Napoleon Hill writes about, and you'll be another one of the millionaires whose inspiration came from a book like that!"

"Along with guidance from you too, of course." Tammy smiled. "Looking back, I can see that you were right. I only read junk before you mentored me to do otherwise. I can't imagine how many great books I could have read instead of the tabloids! But now I am heading in the right direction."

"You are more than going in the right direction, Tammy. You're moving full steam ahead, and I love that about you. I was going over my notes of what we've talked about the past few months and there were some more things I thought we should cover today, if that's OK with you?"

"Absolutely," the student replied, almost before her mentor could finish asking the question.

"I know you've got a lot on your plate at this point in your life. One of the things I've noticed with a lot of entrepreneurs like you is that at some point they begin to lose focus. Like you, they have creative minds and begin to think of what else they can do. They get ahead of themselves. So, what I suggest you do is create your own umbrella of focus."

"What do you mean by that?" Tammy asked. Their coffee order came, and she took a sip of the hot brew.

"Imagine opening a bright yellow umbrella outside when it's raining. The idea is obviously to keep the water off our clothing. When we stay under that umbrella, we will be protected as we focus on keeping as much of ourselves covered as possible. What I want you to do is imagine the umbrella as your focus protector. Underneath it, you keep your fashion design, family, and whatever else is important to you close.

"Now, when outsiders come and offer you the latest and greatest opportunity or program that is important to them—yet it is *not* under your umbrella of interest—you simply say, 'Thank you very much,' and let it roll off the sides of the umbrella just like the rain. In other words, if it's not under your umbrella of focus, don't let it in; don't replace what is important to you.

"I'm mentioning this because you've shared some other ideas with me over the last few months. Hang on to them. Write them down. Keep a file, and fill it with notes—whether it's a physical file or one on your computer. But for now, keep your focus on Keep Smiling Fashions. You've created something that is taking off and requires your absolute full attention.

"I heard the other day that a jet consumes more fuel during the take-off process than during the actual flight. Whether that is the case or not, I'm not sure. But this I do know, your business is in the take-off mode and it needs all your fuel right now!"

"I hear you loud and clear," Tammy said. And she really did. "I'll keep my focus totally on my primary goal."

Emma Walsh began again, "I'm going to share another idea for you to consider. It may seem contradictory to what I just said, though it's really not. I'm sure you've heard the old saying, 'Don't put all your eggs in one basket.'

"A few months ago, I had the opportunity to meet with one of the best-known motivational speakers in the country after he addressed a seminar that I attended. In his presentation, he said that his earnings from speaking represented about one-quarter of his total income. He makes a lot of money speaking but has expanded his thinking to see that if something happened to that source of revenue that his whole financial well would dry up.

"So over the last few years, he has made a lot of money with an internet product he created from his teachings."

"Much of his online income is directly related to his speaking business where people don't have to be in the same physical room in order to buy from him. He has created products related to what he speaks about like books, CDs, DVDs, and more—where he can sell them 24 hours a day in cyberspace. The point of this, Tammy, is simply to plant a seed in your mind about other ways you might be able to add income without losing focus of your primary business. For example, at some point you might lead a seminar for other women who want to leave the kind of job you were in and begin their own businesses, or begin reaching out to new markets that could really enjoy your work. Remember, that's how I made my money. If I only focused on people within my community, I would have gone broke. By reaching out and opening doors throughout the world with TeleWorkout, the world came to me."

"Great point," Tammy affirmed. "I will create my own umbrella and then find ways to make it rain with customers."

"The reason I'm thinking about this is because of what I saw in today's mail." Walsh continued: "There was a story in the newspaper today: 'It's TRUE ... A staggering 66% of Americans do not have enough money to support themselves during retirement.' The big question for each of us is: will we? What are we going to do differently than the 2/3 of the general population? Because, if we aren't doing anything differently than they are, then hang on for a difficult ride down the road.

"But, it doesn't have to be that way. At least, it won't be that way for someone like you, right?"

"Absolutely!" Tammy exclaimed, but with some concern evident in her voice. "You've dropped some great nuggets on me today. I think I need to go away and really concentrate on what you've said."

"Tammy, you have made some very positive decisions. I really believe that your later years are going to be a lot different than most because of those decisions, the actions you've taken, and the work you've done. You aren't going to rely on Social Security. While your former job will provide you with a modest pension, from what you've said, you know it isn't going to be your only source of income when you decide to retire. That is, if you ever do! How many former employees of Enron wish they hadn't put their eggs in *that* corporate basket? Personally, I don't believe Social Security will disappear, but I'm sure not putting all my eggs in the bureaucratic basket either!"

"Then, what are some of the ways I could make money beyond my business?"

"Make sure you pay yourself first, and then learn how to invest. You don't have to do it alone, and I'd be happy to give you the name of the woman who helps guide my investment decisions. Real estate, over the long-term, is normally a wealth-building asset, and maybe someday it's going to make sense to look into buying your own building for your company. That may not be this year; but then again, it may. For many business owners like Savannah Ross, their real estate becomes one of their biggest assets. Other things might include the potential seminars I mentioned or creating information products like books or DVDs. The point, Tammy, is that there are all kinds of possibilities that won't distract you from your own umbrella of interest, so I want you to be keeping your eyes open that you don't end up with only one basket of wealth."

"That all makes so much sense. Every time we get together like this, I can't believe how much you share that I haven't thought about yet."

"Let me tell you, there are a lot of things I don't know yet, either. I can only share some of the things I've been taught along the way. Another of them, by the way, is the need to persevere; to hang in there! Have you had any problems with the business, yet?"

"Oh my goodness, yes!" Tammy responded. She couldn't even begin to list the issues, small and large, that had cropped up on a daily basis.

"Well, just know there will be more—many more—as time goes on. It's impossible to go through life, to build a business, to raise your kids without having problems. The key is to persevere through the problems."

As Emma spoke, she regarded the pupil who sat in front of her. She knew that Tammy's life had been in upheaval for months. Her mom was still very ill, the kids needed her attention and love 24/7, and she was out on a limb with her new business venture.

"The other night I was watching an educational channel on TV and was fascinated by the story I saw about the penguins at the South Pole. They know how to persevere! I was amazed to learn how far inland they go to mate. Once the eggs are laid, the father penguin sits on them to keep them warm through the freezing South Pole winter. During that time the mother penguin trudges back for miles to the sea to fatten up and then many weeks later goes back to take the duty over for the father. These penguins endure more hardship than most creatures ever will but boy do they hang in there! Far too many humans give up at the earliest sign of trouble. Tammy, don't do that. Hang in there!" Emma emphasized her point by repetition.

"I will—I promise, I've got too much to do with my life than to quit when a problem arises. Besides that, I am also doing this for my children. I want them to see me for the person I can be, so that they will do the same."

"Very nice," Emma Walsh said. "The last thing I want to say to you today is simply this—be flexible. Mark Twain said, 'The only person who likes change is a baby with a wet diaper!' I've learned with TeleWorkout the reality that things change quickly; especially with technology. Since so much of the success of TeleWorkout is related to the use of technology, I always have to be aware of change and how that can both positively and negatively affect the business. All I'm saying, Tammy, is to be flexible. Don't get so set in your ways that you won't change and then have that unwillingness to change cost you your business success and your profit margin! Nothing ever remains permanent in life. Everything is subject to change."

"Isn't that the truth."

"Accept that and then allow your mind and attitudes to incorporate changes. For most people that's a very tall order. I don't sense that's the case for you but I want you to be aware of it. Always be sure to review your goals and dreams. If you aren't reaching them, ask yourself what may need to change in order to do so. This way change becomes a friend because it helps you move ahead. Don't change for the sake of change but change for the sake of you!"

"I hear you loud and clear," Tammy said, looking at her watch "I hate to do this but I really need to run as I have an appointment with my banker about increasing my credit line, and you know I need to show up early."

"That sounds important. You should get going, my friend," the mentor encouraged.

"And then I have to go grocery shopping for my mom."

"She's in my prayers, you know. Always."

"Thank you. I'll call you next week so we can schedule our next appointment!" Tammy said, feeling so full of positive motivation and energy.

"Please do that. I have one other thing to share with you that may change your life forever!"

Tammy turned and looked at her, puzzled.

"Tammy, it's nothing bad. It's great, in fact."

"Well, now you have my attention. Should I change my appointment?"

"Absolutely not! I just wanted to make sure you would call." Mrs. Walsh winked.

"You better believe it," the student responded.

That night, after making all of her appointments and putting in a few extra hours reviewing the books at her business, she drove to her ex-in-laws' place to pick up the kids. Sometimes it was only while driving from one place to another that she had quiet time to herself, time to reflect on what was happening in her life and the lives of those she loved.

This time she replayed the conversation with her banker.

It had gone well. Her application was approved without a hitch. The credit line would cover anticipated expenses for another few months if the income from the business did not immediately meet projections. But...

"What if your sales do not exceed, or even meet your budget?" the bank officer had asked her.

"Well..." Tammy felt at a loss for words. She was still learning to keep a positive vision in front of her at all times. Sometimes she felt the negative energies start to overwhelm or black out the positive, light-filled attitude she tried hard to cultivate.

"All I'm saying," the lender advised, "is be prepared for any and every eventuality. And remember, whatever you prepare for, and whatever actually happens—everything is subject to change."

The message couldn't be louder or clearer, could it?

She stayed up late that night, lying in bed after her regular regimen of reading. She kept thinking of her mom.

Pass IT ON

"Tammy, I know you are doing good things with your life. I am so proud of you. I know the kids are, too," Phyllis Conley said.

She looked awful, Tammy thought, after the latest round of chemotherapy that seemed to be having little effect. There was another month of treatment to go, then the oncologist would evaluate the effects of the chemo . . . Could anything save her mother?

God, help her. And help us, she prayed silently. Aloud, she said: "Mom, you have been inspiring me to do my best. I owe all my so-called success to you. The business is catching on, even in this terrible economy. I don't take it for granted, though. Not for a minute."

Her mother patted her hand, as if she were the child she once had been. The older woman said nothing. She was weak. It was difficult for her to spend time with David and Dana with her energy level so low.

"I am learning new lessons every day. I guess I'm a better student now than I was when I was little," Tammy admitted.

Mrs. Walsh had certainly caught Tammy's attention when she said she wanted to share something at their next meeting that might change Tammy's life. In the days that had passed since they met, Tammy had been doing a lot of thinking. Driving back and forth to the hospital and to her mom's house, she thought about how much in her life had already changed since she took the initiative to be mentored.

She could barely believe that, not only had she quit her 40-hour-a-week job at Erickson's, but she had started her own business. There was no way she would have thought that could happen if someone had asked her about a year ago.

Tammy realized that she was happier than ever. Yet, there was so much to be sad and worried about. Her mom, primarily. But she never let herself go all the way down the road to the turn in the distance that she couldn't see.

Not all of her business problems were gone, either, but how she looked at such problems had changed forever. No longer did she see them as roadblocks but rather as opportunities. This, as much as anything, was a huge change in her life.

Every day—rather, late at night—she was reading inspirational and motivational books, and each week she led the mastermind group she began.

As often as possible she was calling and arranging to meet with others in business, men and women, who had accomplished what she someday hoped to accomplish. Mrs. Walsh was right in that so many of these people were more than willing to share so much with Tammy.

All she had to do was ask.

As her business grew, so did the demands on her time and focus. Tammy knew that Emma Walsh had been so correct in their last meeting when she reminded her of the need to be flexible and open to change.

Tammy took this to heart and hired a virtual assistant who took over some of the mundane duties that the new entrepreneur had done by herself for so long. Her virtual assistant arranged the meetings with other business people, sent Tammy email reminders about things on her to-do list and did research on the Internet that Tammy had formerly spent hours doing.

This change, in and of itself, saved her hours and hours of time each month. There was no way in the world that she would have envisioned such a thing if someone had asked her in the grocery store just a few months ago.

During the past week, she even began shopping for a new site for her business with a local commercial real estate agent. She didn't think she was quite ready for the move yet but wanted to be aware of what was available when the right opportunity came along. Real estate had been dropping in price and she figured if the right property came along she might be able to buy it on sale!

She realized that her thinking was so different than it had been. She never even thought she could own a home, much less a business building!

Now she was thinking about how expansion could take place when before she merely wondered what new items she would be selling at the grocery store.

Because of her mastermind group, there were other women in the community who were coming to her for advice about their own dreams. Tammy loved the opportunity to encourage them just as Mrs. Walsh and Julie had encouraged her. It was her opportunity to pass it on.

And maybe the thing that made Tammy the most proud was how her kids were talking about her. She had overhead them on more than one occasion tell their friends about "Mommy owns her own clothing line!"

In fact, the kids had inspired her to look into developing a line of Keep Smiling Fashions just for kids! Her initial research indicated that the kids might have opened the door to a fantastic opportunity that hadn't entered her mind before.

"This new way of living is something I wished I had discovered years ago," Tammy thought to herself. Then she realized that thought was a bit negative sounding like regret and said out loud, "I am so happy to be living the life of my dreams today!"

The reminder alarm sounded on her cell phone. Tammy gathered her things to head to the coffee shop to meet her trusted adviser.

She said to her mother, "I'll be back in about an hour to check in on you. If you feel well enough, we'll take you home tonight to sleep in your own bed."

"That would be nice." Phyllis closed her eyes and smiled wanly.

Tammy leaned over and kissed her on the forehead. She left the room quietly.

She realized she was feeling a little nervous because of how Mrs. Walsh had prepped her for this meeting.

"What in the world more could she share that might change my life more than it already has?" Tammy thought to herself. She summoned up the strength to focus on one thing for the next hour or so. What did Emma Walsh have in mind?

There was only one way to find out.

As luck would have it, both women walked into the coffee shop at the same time, laughing at the coincidence. Of course, they were both twelve minutes early.

They got their coffee and sat down at their usual spot.

"Mrs. Walsh, you've had me on pins and needles since our last meeting. You really messed with me when you set me up like you did!" Tammy laughed nervously.

"Sorry about that. I told you it was positive, remember? The message is quite simple. "

Tammy smiled and placed both her elbows on the table before her, ready to take in the wisdom, as her mentor said just one word.

"Acceptance."

"Of what?" asks the student.

"Of *everything* that happens to you—both good and bad," was her reply. "There is a woman I met years ago named Glenda Lane, a wonderful soul. One day when I was facing challenges of my own, I asked her what I should do. Her answer was clear: 'Just accept it.' Glenda said that, although we cannot control everything that happens to us in life, we can look for the hidden opportunity that lies within difficult circumstances. More important, she said, is to take responsibility for what's happening. That's where the power lies. "

"Power?" asked Tammy.

"Yes," Walsh said. "She says that blaming others gives our power away. On the other hand, taking responsibility allows us to deal with the situation and take control of its outcome."

"That makes sense," Tammy said. "I like this woman already. She sounds like a dynamo."

"To say the least. Glenda is a true champion of life. One time when I was on my own little pity pot, she told me that what was happening to me was a gift, even though it did not look like one at the time. She said, it would be nice if someone offered you an unexpected gift. Yet true appreciation can only be experienced once you *accept* it."

"My gosh that's true!" Tammy exclaimed. "From now on, I will look at things from that perspective. Would you mind if I reached out to her one day, she sounds like someone I should know."

Seeing that Tammy had immediately absorbed this crucial message, the mentor wrote Glenda's information on the back of a napkin and handed it to her pupil. She then excused herself from the meeting.

"When you meet with her, you'll leave inspired. She taught me that resisting the reality of a situation is exhausting and a waste of energy, not to mention the fact that you may also inadvertently be pushing away hidden gems—opportunities—that could alter your life. Often for the better."

Tammy got up to hug Emma, saying, "Thank you so much for everything. I love you."

"See you soon, my dear."

Sitting in the coffee shop alone, after Mrs. Walsh left, Tammy felt an odd sense of freedom, even though she knew it was temporary. She had nowhere to be at this very moment. Her mom was resting at the hospital, the store was running better than ever with the help she'd hired, and her kids were both at school. She had a clean half-hour of free time with nothing planned on her calendar. It felt like hours.

Taking a deep breath in, she basked in the moment of solitude, and lifted her cup to her lips. As much as she enjoyed this simple moment, it suddenly changed when a man voice said

"Excuse me, may I borrow this chair?"

"Of course," Tammy offered in a friendly tone of voice.

"Thank you," he replied. "Hey, don't our kids go to the same school? My name is Ben Garnica."

"Tammy." She extended her hand over the table as she made the introduction. "Oh yes," she added quickly. "I almost didn't recognize you. You look different. Did you get a new haircut or something?"

"I get that a lot," he replied with a smile. "Actually, I used to be a lot larger—110 pounds to be exact."

"Holy smokes!" Tammy exclaimed. "Oh, I'm sorry, did I just blurt that out?"

The two laughed at the outburst, and she could see right away that it was not Ben's first experience with such a reaction.

"No worries. I get that a lot, and actually I love it. I'm proud of what I've done. Trust me it wasn't easy."

"As you can see, I could still lose a bit around the back of my arms. I keep slapping myself in the face every time I wave at someone."

Ben cracked up at the obvious humor and the graphic visualization.

"How did you do it?" she asked.

"From commitment I suppose," he said. "Once I grasped the fact that I needed to stop 'trying' to lose weight and actually committed myself toward the goal, things changed."

"I was just talking to someone about the power of acceptance before I met you, and now you mention commitment. Thinking about it, they are two of the most powerful words around."

"Agreed," Ben said. "Acceptance is huge. I decided to accept the fact that I was responsible for getting to the state I was in. Thus, I was the only one who could get me back to where I saw myself, the size I am today."

"You say you committed toward your goal, what exactly did you do?"

"I broke it down into three steps and promised myself I would follow them."

"Can you share what you did?" Tammy asked as she pulled out a paper and pen to write.

"Sure. It came down to these three things: Realize, rationalize, and then materialize."

"OK, wait, let me get this down." She wrote feverishly. "Realize, rationalize, and then materialize."

"There you go. That will work toward anything: losing weight, moving up in your career, bettering your relationships, anything."

"I don't get it though, can you elaborate a bit?" she asks

"Of course" he responded, settling into the chair beside her. "First you need to *realize*. That means you get honest with yourself. You realize that perhaps you don't have what you want in life and are not getting the ultimate results you desire because the actions you are taking are simply not working.

"Then we need to *rationalize*. This means being honest with the person you look at in the mirror, by holding yourself accountable. Just like you mentioned about acceptance. This is where we need to be in integrity with ourselves and stop pointing fingers at others.

"Finally, once you realize where you are and rationalize that you are the one who got you there, you can then begin to *materialize* the outcome as you envision who you truly are and where you wish to be. We do this by creating a strategy, being open to shift if things don't work, and continue to visualize what the outcome would be like once we get there. In other words, keep your eyes on the prize. "

Writing more quickly than her fingers could move, Tammy worried less about spelling and proper English than about getting the point down on paper so she could remember it later and spend some time reflecting on the message.

"Gosh, Ben, that's fantastic stuff—and congratulations on your achievement. You should write a book on this."

"I appreciate you saying that." He stood to leave.

"You said this approach will work for other things. You mentioned relationships."

"Correct," he said. "I am in a fantastic relationship with a wonderful woman, thanks to applying these same techniques. I've been happily married for years now."

Tammy chimed in, "So what you are saying is that even if we are not in the perfect relationship of our dreams, that we need to realize this fact and stop making excuses for it. Then we need to rationalize that we are the ones who got ourselves into the situation. Now it's up to the individual—me—to no longer accept anything but the best in our relationships."

Turning to leave, Ben looked at his new friend and said, "Maybe *you* should write the book. You pick things up pretty quickly."

Just then, Tammy's cell phone buzzed. She answered the call. It was her mother.

"What's up, Mom?" she asked. It was unusual for Phyllis to call.

"Nothing, dear, just wanted to hear your voice."

"That's all I hear every day," Tammy said. "Nothing special. But it's great to hear you!" She smiled through a tear.

"Great to be heard…but I'm tired. Nighty night." The way she used to say it, when Tammy was a girl.

"Nighty night, Mom."

On the
ROAD TO PAMPER-VILLE

It was difficult for Tammy to get the sound of Ben Garnica's three-point prescription out of her mind.

Looking into the full-length mirror on the back of the closet door, Tammy saw things around her—the good and bad, her mom's illness and her kids' full and happy lives—from a whole new perspective. She was beginning to realize that the greatest asset she possessed was herself. If she could maximize her God-given potential in the ways she was being taught, there was no limit for her and those in her life whom she loved. The clothes she wore were decorated with inspirational messages—the same messages she had internalized—and her new associations were second to none. Now she needed to do more than hear and see the words. She needed to continue to apply all of them.

It was right there. Staring back at her, written in huge letters down the side of her skirt: *Balance.*

Tammy barely kept from laughing at herself as she quickly deduced that, while she was a messenger of this ideal, she could always use a bit more of it in her own daily activity.

That's all it took. A simple "aha" moment. From there, she grabbed the phone and asked for help. It's funny how a woman's mind works. It's so easy for her to offer help to someone else, yet often very difficult for her to ask for it. In this case, she was glad she did. She phoned her in-laws, who were only too happy to keep the kids for an extra few hours. The next call, to one of her mastermind partners, agreed to open the store for her on a volunteer basis, giving her the freedom to get in a little "Tammy Time."

Then she called into her mentor's business, TeleWorkout. With a new session beginning in minutes, she jumped into some sweat pants, placed her phone on speaker and gave the idea a try. She immediately loved it and understood why people around the nation did too.

Physically renewed, she started toward the store. But, before she could get there, another idea crossed her mind. Why hadn't she thought of this before? Pulling the car over, she picked up her cell and asked if her mastermind volunteer could keep the shop running for just a little while more. Without hesitation, her friend agreed, freeing Tammy up to do something that she only reserved for very special occasions.

She called Phyllis. "Mom, I'm on my way to pick you up. Just throw something on, nothing fancy." She didn't listen to her mother's protests, and within a half-hour she and Phyllis walked into Maybelle's Hair and Nail Salon for an unscheduled appointment.

"Well, hi there, stranger," a pleasant-looking woman at the front desk greeted with a Southern drawl. "I haven't seen you in here in forever, sweetheart."

"Hi there back at ya, "Tammy said with a wink. "I decided today was going to be a 'me and my mom' day, can you fit us in?"

"Good for you darlin', come on in. You always have a chair waiting for you here, you know that. And your lovely mother, too."

Walking into Maybelle Jon's salon was a real luxury around these parts. This was where Emma Walsh got her own hair done.

"Here you go," said the store owner as she led Phyllis and Tammy to open styling chairs.

"Thanks, Maybelle, you are such a dear."

Lowering herself into the luxurious leather seat felt reminiscent of ditching school and playing hooky. She knew she should be working, but she also knew that she owed her mom this indulgence—and she wanted to spend the time with Phyllis. Her now-bare feet slipped into warm, soapy water in preparation for a long-awaited pedicure.

Phyllis Conley had a smile on her face, as well. Tammy's mom had lost a lot of weight and had a kind of haggard look to her, but as the minutes passed, she took on a kind of relaxed glow as her own cares melted away.

Letting out the deepest of sighs, Tammy released any thoughts of guilt that were eating at her and melted into her surroundings.

"It's nice, huh?" asked someone beside her.

"Is it ever," Tammy said in a tone of tranquility. "That's why we're here, my mom and me."

"I'm Shelley Radziminski, by the way," said the friendly woman in the next chair.

"Tammy Conley. Nice to meet you. This is just what I needed." She introduced her mother to Shelley. Phyllis went back to reading a magazine, seeming to enjoy herself tremendously.

"I decided to take a break today," Tammy admitted. "I don't know whether I *should* or not, but lately there have been so many voices coming at me from all directions that it's hard to keep everything straight."

Smiling in unspoken agreement, Shelley simply nodded.

"I mean, I'm filled with so many emotions and new lessons, it's almost too much at one time." She didn't say anything specifically about her mother's health, but it came through clearly to Shelley that it was a big part of what was happening.

"Sounds to me like you need a reality check," Shelley said.

"You're not kidding."

"Not in the way that you are probably thinking. I'm talking about listening to your internal voice so you can begin to prioritize from your heart space. I call it a 'heartfelt tune up.'"

Right away, Tammy smiled at the image. She took a deep breath and relaxed in her chair enjoying the bubbles now dancing around her ankles. "I learned how to listen to my inner voice a few weeks ago," Tammy said.

Shelley continued, "Most people make their decisions only from their mind, yet as we know, we are made up of four parts: body, mind, emotion, and spirit."

"I agree with that," Tammy said.

"Well, there you go. You're part of the way there. The secret is to at least be aware of this in order that we can begin to work on it. Most of us, especially in a small town like ours, make most of life choices by what we see on TV or read in the paper. Basically we are 'programmed' or conditioned to believe that we want to drive a certain car, wear a certain designer, or become a millionaire."

"What's wrong with any of those things?" Tammy asked.

"Absolutely nothing... as long as that is what you want and not just what you *think* you want. We need to ask our true selves, are those 'wants' ours? Where did the 'wants' come from? What will they bring you? Who placed those desires in our minds in the first place?

"We do this by sifting through environmental noise, TV ads, inner ego chatter, and the like. When we do, we may find that when we come from a place of spirit, from our heart space, in other words, chances are that we will make a different choice that we originally had in mind. Problem is, most folks live their lives in someone else's chatter and mistake it as their own."

"How did you begin the journey thinking of this, moving in this direction?" Tammy asked, now sitting upright as she eagerly listened.

"For me, it was the discoveries I found while traveling abroad. Once you see places like India, Africa, and Haiti close up, you see that these are actually some of the happiest people on the planet. Once I saw that many don't have even the basic luxury of clean water, or safe shelter, or enough food each day—yet have the biggest and most genuine smiles you've ever imagined—I quickly deduced that happiness doesn't come from the latest pair of designer jeans, it comes from a place deep within."

At this, Tammy's eyes widened, and her ears were open.

"Like I said, most people only tune into the ubiquitous programming all around them: from the conditioning they received growing up in the mass-media and mass-marketing culture. Unfortunately, nearly all our 'wants' are rooted there. Once we look at *why* you desire those 'wants' your perception will begin to change."

"What about when we want success or to become financially independent. The desire for freedom and comfort are real, aren't they?" Tammy asked.

"That's perfect," Shelley responded. "Those are desires of your spirit. This is the most powerful self. Creating from the spirit steers you in the right course. Your mind just helps in making decisions to getting there. For example, if we wish to be here in this beauty salon only so we can look good to others we imitate what we see in the media—and that is coming from our *mind* space. If we find ourselves here because we see ourselves as beautiful and wish to be nice to ourselves because we deserve it, that is coming from a place of *spirit*. Once we begin making all our choices from this perspective, because we want it for ourselves, rather than we want it because what the outsider chatter is telling us, we will begin to find our true freedom."

Turning in her chair, Tammy looked over at her mom. Phyllis Conley was only half-listening to the conversation between her daughter and the other woman. She seemed to be truly content and enjoying the moment…to be present in spirit as well as body.

She wanted to continue the dialogue with her new friend, but before she could get a word out, Mable Jon came up to Tammy and said, "Hey, sugar, Betty is waiting for you in Chair 5. She's got plans to get you all dolled up."

So she thanked Shelley for her insights and went for a long-postponed new hair style. Not because she wanted to look like a celebrity, but now because she felt like one.

"I'll see you over there, Mom," she said to Phyllis.

Once the mani-pedis were finished and their hair styled to perfection, Tammy was filled with a whole new dose of excitement. She dropped her mother off at home and made sure there was a good dinner on the table. The hospice nurse would check in tomorrow, just for good measure. It wasn't time yet, Tammy thought. Phyllis looked surprisingly good and seemed to have a higher than usual energy level this evening.

She said, "You look beautiful."

"Tammy, dear, I *feel* beautiful. Thank you for doing this today. What a nice surprise! It meant an awful lot to me. I'm tired now. I'll have dinner later."

The two kissed good-bye. It felt to Tammy like a last time…but she didn't let herself dwell on that thought.

On the ride into the retail shop, her mind raced around the images of all the things she'd done in life only to look good in others eyes. From high school to today. She had to laugh at herself with the realization that nearly her whole existence had been crafted around what others thought about her. Ironically, after reflection, she also realized that she didn't even stay in contact with the people she was trying to impress in the first place.

It's a strange fact in life that, if we knew how little others really did think of us, we'd probably stop people-pleasing all together.

Entering the store, she relieved her helpful friend with a hug and thanked her for her assistance. "We'll talk more about this at our next mastermind meeting," she promised.

Immediately, she jumped on the phone with her top vendor and asked her to create some new bags for her clientele. From now on, when folks left the shop with their fashions one side would read her trademarked "Keep Smiling" and the other would say, "I bought this for ME!"

All too quickly, it was closing time on the shortest work day in Tammy's life as she had spent most of it in "Pamper-ville," for herself and her mother.

She turned the key to lock the door, and before she could take even two steps toward her car she heard a voice call out, "Don't close up yet!"

Running up, nearly out of breath, a man who was local hero in his own right, reached Tammy and said, "Thank you. Glad I got to you. Listen, I have an idea for your clothing line and want to see what you think."

Steve Rodgers was his name. A former CEO of a major real estate corporation, he had since left corporate America and had started building his own real estate company. His entrepreneurial vision always seemed to be larger and more imaginative than other folks', who could never see outside whatever business box they were comfortable in. And it always served him well in growing and leading business and life.

"What did you have in mind, Steve?" Tammy asked him.

"Tell you what. You don't have to re-open the shop. Let's grab a coffee instead, and I'll explain."

They met in the coffee shop where she so often met with her mentor. Tammy sat in her normal chair. She'd always had great luck in this shop, so naturally, she looked forward to a productive and insightful meeting with Steve.

"I had an idea and a vision awhile back, and wanted to get the phrase and concept out there in the world and the market," Steve said, taking a sip from his brew. "Everyone knows me as the real estate guy. I get that, yet I have aspirations that go much further, deeper and include people in all businesses and walks of life, as well as my world of real estate."

"So, what's on your mind?"

"You've heard the acronym EGO, right?"

"Yes, we say it all the time: 'Edging God Out,'" Tammy replied.

"I have been using my own expression that is the antithesis of this."

"What is it?"

"I created an entire platform around a new terminology that I call IGI."

Cracking up, Tammy repeated his comment questioningly: "New terminology? IGI?"

"Yes." Steve Rodgers had a big grin on his face. "It stands for 'Inviting God In,' or simply, 'Inviting Goodness In.'"

"I love it!" Tammy said—louder than what was customary in the coffee stop. Some of the other customers turned and looked at her. She went on: "Love it, love it, *love* it. Let's do something with that right away. How may I help?"

"That's easy. I know real estate like the back of my hand, and you know your business like the back of yours. I plan to continue building and growing the business I love. And at the same time I roll out these ideas and concepts in workshops and writing, I thought maybe you could use the phrase on some of your clothes next season. In return, I'll share some of the profits for promotion and awareness with you."

"Yes, of course, consider it done. My goodness, that will be a huge hit not only around here, but with my international clients, too." Tammy's international business had just begun to gain some traction. This was "tailor-made" for that clientele.

"I was hoping you'd say that. I'm also working on some writings, blogs, videos, and getting some seminars together around the idea. I think it's quite powerful. And the concepts can be used in business or spiritual venues depending on the group—and how the wording is phrased. So, it does have universal appeal.

"I'm going to start printing it on all my marketing and promotional communications, business cards, and brochures. In fact, my niece, who is a Broadway performer, has already created a theme song for it.

"In today's economy, and with all our current governmental and business changes, I think most of us are trying for a bit less EGO than we used to have, and are slowly finding a way toward IGI. So, I hope to share what has been the focus in my life and help others make it work for them, too. I appreciate any support and promotion you can offer to see this through."

Tammy was a bit taken aback that a successful CEO and growing-business owner was coming to her to share his ideas and partner with her. Wait till Mrs. Walsh hears about this! Wait till I tell my mom, too…she'll be so proud.

The two continued the discussion for a while, until Tammy looked at her watch and jumped up from her chair. "Oh my, Steve. I'm late. I love the terminology, the whole idea—and, yes, I will help. I think this could be a huge success for us." She dug into her purse for her keys, even as she said, "I'll be in touch soon. I have to run." The two hugged good-bye before Tammy bolted out the door.

Judgement DAY

Arriving right on time for her next appointment, she felt a little bit off. For nearly every meeting these past several months, she was early. Punctual, or even on time, for her now meant she was late.

"Hello, gents," Tammy greeted as she entered the prestigious Boa. The fanciest restaurant in town was the venue of choice for anniversaries, weddings, and prom night. Taking the counsel of her mentor, she had decided to ask Emma to help her schedule this meeting with the two smartest business people she knew.

Joe Barbieri was a legend in these parts for the mark he had made in the food industry. Over the years, he had helped create some of the largest international brands and take them to a whole new level of success. Sitting next to Joe was Roger Bishop, a renowned expert in the behind-the-scenes world of human resources and business development.

Tammy knew that for her business to grow, she would need to come from a place of spirit and heart. She also understood that it would take action, leadership, and guidance from people who had already paved the way. She hoped they might show her the path to getting there.

"Hello, young lady." Roger rose and politely pulled out her chair.

Joe spoke up, as well: "Emma Walsh asked us to meet you to see if we may be of assistance in some way."

"I am very grateful." It was a tad bit different for Tammy, being in the company of such dynamic male figures. She also knew that their perspective toward personal achievement would likely be a little different from what she had been hearing lately. "As you have heard, my business is really growing lately—in a huge way, to be honest. We have already outgrown our local market and are doing almost 62% of our business out of state and 11% internationally. The question is, now that things are moving in this positive direction, I may need to grow my staff. Do you have any suggestions for me?"

Pulling out a document from his brief case, Roger said, "There are many suggestions and ideas." Showing her a 3"x5" laminated card with text written on it, he went on, "This is what I refer to as my 'play list for success.'"

"Play list?" Tammy said.

"Yes, just as a coach would have a play book or list of his most successful plays when he is coaching a sports team. I realized I could use something like that to help remind me of certain moves I could use when navigating the game of life. To date, I must have given out over a thousand of these. Here you go."

Joe added: "That's a great idea, Roger. I never knew you carried something like that around with you."

"The first thing on this list refers to exactly what I was asking about," Tammy said as she read aloud:

Things change over time – keep up with change.

"I think I'm doing that pretty well," she said. "I've learned that *everything* is subject to change. Keeping up with it—Mrs. Walsh has me set up with a fantastic web developer who has me able to take orders from people anywhere around the globe. What's really amazing is that no matter where someone comes from, the best-selling inspirations are always the same. I find they really respond to the word *respect*."

"There you go." Roger looked from Joe to Tammy, encouraging her. "Look at this list. So many people forget the basics of life and forget that there is—or can be—a play list to refer to. As you read through the list, you will see that they are very simple messages which hold tremendous value when applied. For example, coming from a strong HR background, the one common denominator I found is that people simply want to be treated as such...as *people*. Just like the point you made about respect."

"Couldn't agree more with both of you," Joe said. "Over the years, I have seen first-hand the power of treating people not as you want to be treated, but the way *they* wish to be treated. It is all about respect. Although everybody has different individual goals and dreams, we all have something in common. We desire the opportunity to make those dreams a reality. Every company I have ever owned or worked for has seen the amazing benefits of simply giving a 'little' bit more than is expected. In return they have created some of the strongest support systems and employee base ever imagined."

"You are spot on," Roger Bishop added. "The secret to helping you grow your business is never to lose site of the people who help you succeed. Besides being good business, it is the right thing to do."

"Thank you," Tammy said as she lifted the index card. "These are going to be great tips, I can already see."

"And don't forget the Golden Standard," Joe Barbieri said, looking squarely at Tammy.

"You mean the Golden Rule?" she said.

"I refer to it as the Golden Standard, because everyone should live their life by one simple philosophy and standard of practice. You have to have integrity. Short and simple. Do as you say, say as you do. That is the one standard—the Golden Standard—that has never changed in my life and although I am sure I could have made more bucks over the years by cutting corners, employee pensions, et cetera…I never would. On my tombstone all I want it to say is: 'Joe's word was always gold.' I think that would be a wonderful way to be remembered."

With a smile brighter than firelight, Tammy stared at Joe with a loving expression. She could see the emotion and dedication this man had for his mission.

Adding a new point of his own, Roger said, "Joe, I really appreciate you saying that. Like I mentioned, almost all the greatest insights are time-tested, age-old wisdoms that have slipped away somehow. That's why it's so important to keep your play list with you at all times. Any time you feel challenged, pull it out—chances are you will get the direction you need right from that card.

"Another great point to remember—and, Joe, I'm sure you will agree with this—is to always make up your mind about someone or something on your own. Don't pre-judge."

Joe jumped in: "Oh yes, that is a great one. Easy to say, tough to do—yet imperative if you are to succeed at anything."

"Why is that?" Tammy inquired.

Roger answered: "Because you never know who it is you are going to cross paths with. For example, my wife owns a motorcycle accessory business. Many times the people who buy from her, the average person would probably judge as grubby, or an outcast. The funny thing is that most of these people come to her on their day off from their regular jobs as policemen, firemen, pastors, or accountants. Point is, you never should judge someone by their appearance, education, or anything else for that matter."

"I get that," Tammy said. "Naturally, I teach that lesson to my kids, yet in real life I could probably apply the action a bit more myself. So many times when out-of-towners come into the store, I figure they are just 'lookie loos.' Fact is, they always seem to turn out to be my best clients. Go figure."

The two men smiled at her as she continued. "Oh, I love this one...

Hold people accountable.

"It seems that lately, I have picking been up the slack for others when they promise to do something. Perhaps I need to be more direct, and not be such a push over. Like you said Joe, do as you say and say as you do. If they say they will do it, I should hold them to it."

"Now you're talking," Roger said. "Be firm, and be fair I always say. The easiest way to do this is set the boundaries from the beginning. Don't be afraid to have them sign an agreement that states the terms, time, and consequences."

"I did that with my oldest not too long ago," Tammy said. "When they said they would do chores around the house, I had them sign a 'promise note' and if they did not finish what was agreed upon, they lost TV privileges. Of course they finished, but if they didn't, it would have been easy to just hold up their signed agreement and unplug the set. What could they say? They knew the deal going in."

Joe looked at Roger and gave him a wink, knowing that Tammy was catching on quickly.

"How we do something, is how we do everything," Joe said. "And when we do what's right, the right things happen. Past sayings I know, and still as relevant as ever. Remember this: Being authentic and having integrity will never go out of style."

Roger applauded the moral before continuing his thought.

"There will be times in life and business that your word may be all that you have. It's the best collateral." Roger pointed to a line on the card. "Like Joe and I are saying, by doing what's right you will *always* be proud of yourself and what you do."

Reading the notes from the card that Roger had created and to which she had added points from Joe, she said: "OK, I think I got it. Use this card as a reminder of a playbook for success."

- *Always apply the Golden Standard.*
- *Respect is the key that opens hearts and doors.*
- *Make up your own mind, don't judge.*
- *Hold others and yourself accountable.*
- *Our word is our best collateral.*
- *Integrity never goes out of style.*

After their meal was finished, the three rose and said their farewells. Both men offered to meet with Tammy any time she felt challenged, and they exchanged their contact info.

Walking with them, she turned and said, "I truly appreciate your guidance, insights, and reminders. The best way I can show my appreciation is by applying what we spoke about. So—consider it done!"

Before she could call it an early evening, she had one more stop to make. This one to cap off the day. A trip to the local ice cream store, where she would treat herself to pure dietary decadence.

"A double scoop of love," she called to the server behind the counter. Being a long-time regular, they knew exactly what she meant: One scoop vanilla, one scoop chocolate, and then a drizzle of caramel on top.

Sitting in the car, eating her frozen creation, she caught a glimpse of herself in the rearview mirror. She began laughing aloud at her self-created fear of what others would think, seeing her eating her desert. "I feel like a drug-user or something," she laughed aloud to herself.

Out of the corner of her eye, she saw another woman in another car with her back turned, enjoying her treat in the same fashion. Deciding to make a new friend, she calmly walked over and said, "Hi, my name is Tammy. I see you and I have something in common."

There was no response. Thinking the just hadn't heard her, Tammy repeated: "Hi there."

Again, no response.

At this moment Tammy became a bit upset at the rudeness of this woman. Heck, she wouldn't ever turn toward her or acknowledge she was even there.

Instead, the stranger just kept typing away in her cell phone, obviously texting someone.

Before Tammy could leave she tried one more time. "Excuse me, I'm right here behind you. Are you OK? Do you need something?"

For the third time, there was no response from the stranger. Just a continued onslaught of tapping buttons on her phone.

That was enough for Tammy. With no reaction, she turned and headed back to her car in a huff. "How rude is that?" she said loud enough for the other person to hear. Sitting in her car, she started fuming. Upset at how anyone could not even give her the time of day. "It was a perfect day and now it's ruined" she thought. "I should really give that lady a piece of my mind."

And just then, another car pulled up. The driver got out and walked to the texting woman and did something she had only seen in movies. The new person began speaking to her in sign language.

The woman with whom Tammy had been so furious a moment before turned to the new arrival, hugged him and started signing back. You could see the obvious relief on her face that the other person was there when they opened the hood of the car and went inside to take a look. Instantly, Tammy realized that she was texting people for help from her phone, and simply could not hear Tammy or anything else.

"Well, what do you know?" Tammy asked herself. "I just got a lecture from two wonderful men teaching me the importance of not judging people, and here I am minutes later doing just that."

As she neared the two standing over the engine, the woman whom she had attempted to communicate with before smiled and signed, "Hello."

Feeling a bit silly, Tammy explained to the woman what had just happened. Fortunately, the stranded woman could read lips and got the gist of the story. Lifting her cell phone, the deaf woman showed it to Tammy with an expression as if to ask whether she had one, too.

Tammy handed over the device, and the stranger typed in her number and sent a greeting.

"My name is Bridget Bonheyo," it read. "Nice to meet you."

Tammy typed back, "I'm Tammy, and I'm sorry for misjudging the situation. I could have called for help 15 minutes ago."

Bridget signed, "It's OK." Even though Tammy had never seen this before, knew what she meant.

Tapping the digits Tammy asked, "I know many people around here and have never seen you before. Are you passing through?"

"Actually, no. I moved here a few weeks back and love the place, everyone is so friendly."

"Except for me, of course."

Bridget laughed. "You are too cute, and I love that outfit. Where did you get it?"

Pulling out a business card Tammy handed it over and point to herself, mouthing, "Me."

Tammy was amazed how simple it was to communicate, especially having the use of her phone. The real pleasure was seeing what a wonderful woman Bridget appeared to be.

"I borrowed this car from a neighbor. Mine is still in the shop," Bridget typed. "Darned thing stalled on me."

After the new arrival couldn't seem to get it started, Tammy offered Bridget a ride home.

Once they get to her place, which was twice the size of her own, Tammy, was invited in. They sat and shared some tea. Bridget went to get her hearing aid as Tammy was typing into her phone, "This is a great property. It's the Oakdale property. I went to school with a gal who grew up here. How did you get it? You must be doing pretty well."

Shyly, Bridget said, "By asking for help."

Motioning the international "huh" shrug, the home owner continued, only this time in a regular speaking voice. "When I was new in business, I realized the importance of help. On the same note, the more times I reached out, the more offers to assist came in. I believe our success or failure is in direct proportion to the ability to reach out for guidance."

Taken back by the message and Bridget's sudden ability to speak, Tammy's eyes opened. She typed back: "I get that and agree. And, hey, you can speak. How come?"

Bridget said, "I speak better with my hearing aid, especially when working or interacting with hearing people. By reading lips, I pick up pretty much everything." She winked at Tammy and finished her thought: "And oh yes, one more lesson, don't judge a book by its cover."

Understanding the sarcasm, Tammy laughed and connected palms with Bridget in a "high-five."

She mouthed, "I think we are going to be life-long friends."

Bridget smiled and nodded in agreement. "I think so too."

Tammy returned home and called her in-laws. It seemed like the thousandth time she had done so. "Can you bring the kids by for me?" There were unexpected tears in her eyes as she said it. It was a simple thing, but it seemed so wrong and so sad—that Dana and David weren't already right here at her side. That she was so busy with work and care-giving for her own mom that her children, as much as she loved them, were almost like little strangers to her.   When Mary Beth and Felix Hartman brought them in, Tammy Conley rushed to her children and grabbed them both and squeezed them with all her strength.

"Mommy!" Dana said, barely able to breathe.

Little David looked at his mother as if she were nuts.

Mary Beth said, "Uh, Tammy, I think they're hungry. I'm sorry—we just can't keep these little ones filled up."

Just then her cell phone rang. Immediately Tammy's heart skipped a beat. She hoped it might be her new friend Bridget, but it wasn't. She recognized the number of her mother's hospice nurse. She listened to the voice on the line.

"Yes," she said simply. It was the news she had dreaded. It had finally come.

Her ex-mother-in-law said, "Are you OK? Tammy?"

Tammy could barely hear her former mother-in-law, Mary Beth, the kids' grandmother . . . now their *only* grandmother.

Dandelions

Waking up, feeling weary, tired, and full of grief, Tammy decided to call her mastermind group together. Who better to be with at this moment in her life?

She spent the day finalizing funeral plans, arranging for her ex-husband to share responsibility for the kids for the next 24 hours, and closing down the retail store for a few days. She'd been running on fumes, but surprisingly, she felt little of the chaos that such an upheaval usually brings into one's life. Tammy felt centered and at peace, as though she felt her mom's presence at her side...

At the kitchen window, as she stood over the sink to wash a few dishes, keeping her mind focused, distracted from dark feelings of regret and remorse over her mother's passing. Tammy looked out and saw that her yard was suddenly filled with dandelions. They had not been there the day before…or had they? When was the last time Tammy had looked out at her yard or been out there playing with the kids?

Her mom had loved dandelions, considered them her favorite flower and always joked that they weren't "weeds." "Kids are weeds," she used to say. "They always sprout up where you don't want them, and they're always under foot!"

That brought a smile to Tammy's face.

She heard the kids in the living room. Tim was there, too. He had dropped everything to be there for them—and out of respect for Phyllis. Tammy was grateful beyond words. He had encouraged her to spend some time with friends this evening.

In attendance at the mastermind meeting later were the four women who had become her closest and dearest friends and colleagues—each of whom was all on a similar life path. Even though each had already made a mark in a different arena, they were equally committed to assisting one another along the process.

As they gathered, they offered Tammy their condolences, sharing hugs and tears.

"Hello, ladies." Tammy welcomed them and opened the meeting. She kept a box of tissues handy, just in case the tears returned. "Over this past year I have seen some changes, and I don't mean small ones. Each of us has grown and learned things that have affected our lives in a wonderful way," she said.

The others nodded silently in agreement. They all admired how Tammy was handling herself and were amazed at her resiliency.

"One of the first lessons I learned was about sifting through what everyone was throwing at me and keeping the nuggets that worked. The 'hand of sand' suggestion. The idea was to say thank you for the input that did not work for me and let it slip through my fingers, while keeping the portions that applied toward what I was striving for and would help me succeed along the journey. Now that our companies are growing and our relationships have hit an all time high, I thought it would be nice to share a few of the nuggets we've kept for ourselves and write them here in a notebook. This book will stay with the group, and although our members may change over the years as we move on, or the group expands, the book will become the focal point for all that become part of our mastermind team. Past, present, or future."

"We are the first to participate," said LeAnne Williamson. "How can there be a past?"

"Great question," Tammy responded. "I have asked my mentors Emma and Julie to be the first to contribute to the wisdom book, and they agreed. Considering they were the ones who inspired our meetings in the first place, I thought it would be appropriate for them to be the first to write in it. "

"You're always coming up with something," said Maile Andrus-Price, the woman in the group with a perpetual smile.

Valerie Sheppard said, "It's a continuum, I think. We are connected to both the past and the future here this evening."

The final member, Tina Marie, an outspoken woman with immense wisdom of her own to share, asked: "What did Emma say?"

"She said that basically the future of leadership will have a 'retro' look and feel."

"Let me see that." LeAnne took the book and read aloud, "Emma writes: 'In my humble experience, the secret to success, leadership and relationships is determined by one simple trait, summarized by one word, *authenticity*. Understanding that the quality of our associations is equal to our quality of communication. Just as we were taught years ago from history books, the more we can purely be ourselves, speak from the heart and show our authentic selves, the easier it will be to gain new friends and alliances. People want to see us—flaws and all—for who we are, and not just an image we portray. Real authenticity is the code to unlock our desires. It doesn't matter who you are or where you're from, success is a byproduct of simply being our true selves.'"

LeAnne handed the book over to Tina Marie and offered her applause for the great message, saying, "Excellent!"

Valerie asked, "What does it say?"

Tina Marie said, "On this next page, Julie Browne has a thought of her own. She says: 'Don't be afraid of your street smarts. The life lessons we experience in the real world, out on the street, so to speak, will be far more powerful than those we will ever get from school. We all understand that knowledge is power. Yes it's true, yet it's the application of that knowledge that separates the rich from the poor, the dreamers from achievers. Chances are you already know everything you need to know to make it in this world. Stand in front of a mirror and ask yourself, if you were going to give yourself counsel on what you should be doing, what would that be? Then ask yourself, and be honest…Why aren't you doing it?'"

"Another great point," Maile interjected. "What did you have in mind for us?" she asked the mastermind group's leader.

"I thought we could add the key points and messages that have affected us most. I took the liberty of placing the ones I thought to be most powerful from my journey, and then I thought each of you could add to it as well, by sharing what main core principal or story had made a positive impact in the way you live your life today."

Tina Marie asked, "What do you have so far?"

Tammy lifted the book and said, "Basically I wrote some great bullet points to remind us of the morals to the stories we have shared. Here are some of the main ones that I've gathered over time." She read aloud:

From Bill Frase: Avoid giving yourself a "But Freeze." Come from a place of freedom rather than fear.

From Gavin Keilly: Making sure everyone walks away happy is the only way to do business. And it's profitable.

From Savannah Ross: Discover what would make you run through fire. In all aspects of life, personal, professional, etc.

From Iris Hirsch: Write your own life's story. Use a big eraser and color outside *the lines.*

From Ron Freeman: Bring others together for joint ventures, share the profit and risk—create a win-win prospect for all.

From Alex Szinegh: Right script, wrong day. Don't get talked out of your dreams.

From Barbara Pitcock: Envision your success. Then get out of God's way.

From Glenda Lane: Accept everything *that comes your way as a gift.*

From Roger Bishop: Make a play list of simple messages. They will always be there for you to draw inspiration from.

From Joe Barbieri: The Golden Standard. Everyone should live their life by one simple philosophy and standard of practice.

From Holly Eburne: Look For Good. Our actions reflect our results.

From Valerie Sheppard: Acknowledge the truth of who I am. This is the key that will give me the freedom to become the best me I can be.

From Roxane Marie Schwabe: The power of the inner source. This allows us to listen to ourselves and tune out negative "monkey-mind" chatter.

From Ben Garnica: Realize, rationalize, then materialize. Keep your eyes on the prize.

From Mike Corradini and Sam Khorramian: Synergy creates something many times stronger than any one single entity.

From Desiree Doubrox: Bringing like minds together in a positive, supportive environment empowers one and all.

From Shelly Radziminski: Know why you want the things you want. Does it come from a spiritual place?

From Steve Rodgers: IGI means "Inviting God In" or "Inviting Goodness In." It is just the opposite of EGO: "Edging God Out."

From Bridget Bonheyo: Success or failure is in direct proportion to the ability to reach out for guidance.

When she finished reviewing several of the wisdom nuggets she had acquired, Tammy said, "As you see, I already have Valerie in the book. And now you other three ladies, I would like you to add your own little gems in here. If you could share any one message that has affected your life in the greatest manner, what would that be? Who would like to go first?"

"I would." With a sincere smile, LeAnne raised her hand, as if she were in a classroom. "Coming from a strong HR background myself, I can really appreciate where Roger and Joe were coming from. So much so, that I have been waiting to share a little surprise with you gals." Pulling out four copies of a bound manuscript, she handed each of her peers a copy.

"As we all know, Abraham Maslow said that everyone works from a hierarchy of needs. Considering that most of our time is spent in the workplace, as in life, that same hierarchy of needs applies, as well. One of the primary jobs of leadership is to find out what their workforce needs to progress in their position—and then find a way to make that position a career for them. This is how people can make a better life for themselves and their families. Factors such as health benefits, savings plans, clubs, matching, 401K's, and the like are just teasers to get workers to come take a look see. Yet they do not compel them to stay.

"When an environment is created with a shared reality, where everyone has a role, knows his or her role, and can be successful in that role...*that* is how to keep great people. They will then take care of your clients and customers the same way you take care of them."

"It would be hard to disagree with that observation," Tina Marie stated. "What are these?"—referring to the documents that had been handed out.

"This, friends," LeAnne continued, "is my book. It is going to be released soon and is going to set the industry on fire."

"What's it called?" Valerie asked.

"That's the best part. Considering people know me as being a bit, let's say, outspoken—" The women laughed at the obviousness of her statement. "I came up with a title that would say everything it needed to get the point across."

"So what's the title?" Maile reiterated the question.

"How about this: *Your Service Sucks, and Your Competition Loves You For It.*"

Everyone burst out laughing at the cleverness of the title and the great branding.

"OK, my turn," Maile Andrus-Price offered. "I can truly appreciate where you are headed with that, LeAnne. In my case, and coming from more of a metaphysical, spiritual side, I feel the most important message to share is about realizing our own worth. LeAnne, you have inspired me. I think I may write a book one day on this topic as well.

"We need to share the message, and it's appropriate for the masses because there are millions of women out there who are turned on, tuned in, and tantalized by the prospect of validating their own worth. I am one of them! I asked my husband the other day, what could he do to know his own value or worth? He said, 'I don't understand the question.' I laughed so hard, because it was such a classic response. It may be a stereotype, yet I think women are plagued by doubt about their worth. While men don't necessarily even think about it. And I believe I have a system to help women discover this truth about themselves."

Tammy was deeply intrigued and said, "Tell us more."

Tina Marie chimed in: "Yes, tell us, Maile, what did you find?"

"I didn't expect to be sharing this tonight," Maile admitted, feeling a bit of stage fright. She reached in her purse and pulled out a wrinkled paper that she had been working on—crossing things off and rewriting other thoughts. "I call it my 'BE-attitudes.'"

"BE-attitudes?" Valerie queried.

"Yes. I found that when women followed these five simple steps when faced with questioning their value, they felt better once they completed them."

"OK, so what are they?" Tammy prompted.

Maile reviewed each one.

> • *BE Still. There is knowing in the stillness. Anytime I get still, I feel connected to something bigger than me.*
> • *BE Thankful. Gratitude expands your vision and opens you up to more blessings.*
> • *BE Authentic. This allows trust in self and from others. (Just as Mrs. Walsh wrote about)*
> • *BE Forgiving. It frees you to move forward. Also, Be For Giving—service generates value on both sides.*
> • *BE Focused. This brings the commitment you need to achieve your goals and grows self*

confidence, which makes you feel good about yourself because you can't feel good about yourself without knowing you are of worth.

Tammy and the others smiled brightly at each other with pride in their mastermind partner and friend. They agreed to talk more in depth about these BE-attitudes at their next meeting.

"What about you, Tina Marie, do you have something?" Tammy then said.

"Naturally," she responded with confidence. "As you know, over these past few years I have been doing my internet radio show. My favorite part about doing it is the ability to meet new people and discover new thoughts. It seems that nearly every time I invite someone on, they say yes. So much so, I expect it whenever I pick up the phone. One day however, when I was attempting to book a guest, I got my first negative response. You see, I was so used to hearing yes that I simply didn't even react to it. I just kept talking to them as if they had given me an affirmative. Before I figured out they were turning me down, they seemed to like my eagerness, retracted their response and agreed to come on after all.

"That's where I discovered something I call 'Living to the Power of YES!' The way I see it, the bigger we go, the better chance we have for success. "

"How do you *go bigger*?" said Maile.

"That's easy: Go for the NO and get the YES. Meaning, don't be afraid to ask for the things we want in life, in fact 'know' it's OK to go for the gold. Ask for what you really want to be so large that you almost expect a NO. What you will find is that at the end of the day, chances are there is a YES in there just waiting for you to arrive."

Maile gave Tina Marie a warm look, like she had just delivered a message that was meant for her at exactly the right time.

"Remember this," Tina Marie continued, "NOs can be good things. Actually, let me rephrase that. There is true value in discovering our NOs. A NO is only a block, an obstacle keeping you from a sale, a date, or even an appearance on my show. Usually when we find ourselves at this point, and faced with the challenge, is when we need to do as you mention, Maile, and quiet ourselves as see what that block is."

"Love it!" Valerie affirmed.

"Again, once we 'know' what the NO is, it is then and only then that we may address it or simply move right over the top. In other words, we have to go for the NO or 'know' how to get the YES."

Maile took out another paper and began writing down the description, as Tina Marie continued: "What if you could really have the life you have always dreamed of, yet *you* were the only obstacle in the way? On every occasion, ask yourself, 'What am I to know in this moment?'

"And then be still and listen." She summed it up for the masterminds this way:

- *Find your NO.*
- *Reveal your KNOW.*
- *Go for the gold, and get that YES!*

The viewing for Phyllis Conley took place the following evening at the same local funeral home where Tammy's dad, Jim, had been waked. All those memories flooded Tammy's mind and heart, yet she felt the same strange sense of peace—and even happiness that her mom was no longer suffering. Phyllis was at last, herself, at peace. And she and her beloved husband Jim, Tammy's father, were reunited.

Tammy's sister, Jane, and her family were there too. Although they had not been close in recent years, they had talked on the phone almost every day for the past several months during their mom's illness—and Jane had been able to visit twice and spend a good amount of time with Phyllis.

This was the first occasion for Dana and David to meet their cousins, Jane's kids, who were a bit older and really "cool," according to Dana...The family, so long apart, had come together to mourn and to support one another.

Tammy and Jane, along with their kids, sat together in the front pew of the church the following morning at the funeral. The church could hold about 250 to 300 worshipers, and Phyllis' simple casket stood at the front. As the service began, Tammy looked around. What she saw astounded her and lifted her heart: The place was filled to capacity, with every seat occupied and at least three or four dozen others standing.

She recognized each face in the crowd of mourners. They were family friends, customers from Erickson's Grocery, her former bosses and colleagues there, customers from her retail store, her dear mastermind group, the leaders she had met with along the way—every one of them who had shared their wisdom with her. There were childhood friends she hadn't seen in years, her former boyfriend Rob, her own employees who had made Keep Smiling Fashions such a customer-service phenomenon, and even Bridget Bonheyo, her deaf friend who had taught her so much in such a short time.

After a while, she could barely see anything or anyone, for the tears welled up in her eyes. She hugged David and Dana even more closely to her, one on each side.

Emma Walsh sat a few pews behind Tammy and her family members. The mentor merely smiled and nodded her support and love. Words were not needed. And standing at the back, among so many others who had come out to pay their respects, was Julie Browne, her super-successful girlfriend, mentor, and model. As always, Julie looked elegant but not overdressed in a simple black dress and necklace of pearls. She lifted her gloved hand in a brief wave, then touched her heart.

The pastor said a few words to open the funeral service and offered a prayer. Then he said: "Ladies and gentlemen, friends of Phyllis Conley and the deceased's family, we have a special gift from those who knew and loved Phyllis so much. Please remain seated as the gift is presented."

Within a few minutes, as Tammy sat back in awe, bouquets and displays of *dandelions* were brought in and placed up front in the sanctuary and around the walls, until the entire church seemed covered in bright yellow and green.

"Mommy, Mommy, look!" It was Dana, excitedly watching as the dandelions filled every bit of space available in the sanctuary in golden splendor. "Grandma's very favorite flowers!"

The fragrance of the wild weed-flowers filled the church. Tammy could barely see through her tears. She could not speak.

Everything had changed. Her mother was gone. New friends filled her life. Her kids were growing—yes, like weeds!—and all too fast. The predictions her mentors had made about her life were coming true. What was next? What lay ahead for Tammy?

"Change," she could hear Emma Walsh saying...even though the word was only in her mind. The sight and smell of the dandelions, Dana and David's childlike wonder in this special moment, the sight of all her friends, the pastor's words of comfort, her sister's hand on her own—all was different, yet familiar and real.

Everything is subject to change, she thought. And what a powerful thing that is. She envisioned her mom smiling down from heaven at the hundreds and hundreds of dandelions amid which her daughter sat with a tearful smile of gratitude on her face.

Co-author Biographies

Alex Szinegh is an immigrant from Hungary with a 10th-grade education—but a lot of "street smarts." He has built several successful businesses. Alex is an award-winning author, speaker, trainer, and performance coach. He conducts training and speaking engagements and personally coaches, individuals, and organizations to success. Alex tells it like it is.   Alex is happily married to his wife, Gina, and they have 8 children and 8 granchildren. To book Alex for an event or coaching contact him at: **alexszineghcoach@aol.com**

Barbara Pitcock is truly an American success story with humble beginnings from a small town in Kansas where she overcame many obstacles and adversities to become one of today's most sought after-speakers who trains and inspires people to become all they can be—as the victor, not the victim. Her book, *No Guts—No Story!* shares how she was once a bankrupt beautician and became a multimillionaire working from home. Break through with Barb Pitcock at **www.barbpitcock.com**

Ben Garnica is a Southern California native who moved to San Diego in 1996 to pursue his entrepreneurial desires. With his background of success in business and personal health, Ben shares his methods and strategies through speaking and personal coaching. He has developed a passion for helping others achieve their personal, business, and health goals. Ben can be reached at **bengarnica@yahoo.com**

Bill Frase is an expert at helping individuals and organizations recognize and release the unconscious fears that are holding them back from success. He does this as a professional coach, speaker, and author. Bill may be contacted at **Bill@BillFrase.com**

Bridget Bonheyo is the founder and CEO of SportsMX, an international Web-based sports news service that caters to deaf and hard-of-hearing community. Bridget is a long-time avid supporter of women's movements and the establishment of advocacy agencies for abused deaf women and children. Contact at: **bbonheyo@sportsmx.com**

An entrepreneur since age 12, **Desiree Doubrox** has always been the founder/owner of her own businesses. After a successful career in real estate, she devoted herself to empowering other women. Taking the message beyond just networking, Desiree hosts a weekly Web TV show and a weekly Web radio show and has written book, *Thoughts of An Empowered Woman*. Her company, An Empowered Woman, Inc., offers coaching, monthly mastermind meetings, and an online Women's Business Resource Center which includes businesses as far as South Africa, France, Canada, and the Philippines.
www.anempoweredwoman.com

Gavin B. Keilly is founder and CEO of GBK (www.gbkproductions.com), a luxury lifestyle gifting and special events company, specializing in entertainment marketing integration. GBK is dedicated to giving each client customized marketing options with high quality and tailor-made services. GBK has taken part in Oscars, Emmys, Golden Globes, Backstage at the BET, GLAAD Awards, Sundance and Cannes film festivals—and the list goes on. Over the last three years, GBK has donated more than $3 million in products, cash, and services to charity. **www.gbkproductions.com**

Glenda Lane is a wellness coach/physical therapist with 20 years of experience. She helps people feel "alive" by achieving healthy and balanced lifestyles. Glenda inspires others to "shine brightly" and live authentically in alignment with their aspirations. She lives in Edmonton, Canada with her husband Tom and daughter Sophia. Glenda can be reached at **www.glendalane.ca**

Holly Eburne is a health and wellness coach, a writer and a speaker. For 29 years Holly has been a physical therapist traveling around the world with Canada's national athletes. Since Holly's husband was diagnosed with dementia in 2007, she has been focusing on coaching and teaching caregivers how to live well and "look for good"—regardless of the circumstances. If you are a caregiver and want to feel less overwhelmed and more hopeful, go to **www.hollyeburne.com**

Iris Hirsch is a founder of BASECAMP International Coaching, an organization committed to helping

individuals reach their full potential in all aspects of their journeys through life. Launched in conjunction with Iris' son, Josh, BASECAMP is a reflection of her deep belief in people power. Iris' advice to others is simple and straightforward. "I believe you write your own life story. So write in pencil. Bring a large eraser. And color outside of the lines." She can be reached through her Website at:
www.thebasecampexperience.com

Joe Barbieri: His word is gold. He can be reached at **joe@jbassociates1.com**

To say that **LeAnne Williamson's** career has been varied is an understatement. After holding management positions in the automotive industry and real estate, LeAnne is as passionate about sharing her knowledge and life experience as she is about working with people. An entrepreneur, certified coach, professional speaker, and author, in 2003 LeAnne started Your Success Coach, Inc., a company designed to educate and train individuals and businesses to follow their passions and achieve superior results. **leanne@theyscgroup.com**

Maile Andrus-Price was born in Tokyo, Japan and returned with her family to Hawaii when she was two. She is an RN, author, speaker, and entrepreneur. Her purpose is to assist others to reconnect with their divine worth. She currently resides on the island of Oahu and can be reached at:
www.thedaoofdonuts.com

Mike Corradini and **Sam Khorramian** are international speakers and serial entrepreneurs who have mastered the art of synergy. Individually, both Mike and Sam have launched and grown a number of successful companies from a clothing brand to a lead-generation company, and most recently a national real estate investment firm. Their partnership has given birth to a number of multi-million dollar businesses that resulted in them being featured in Yahoo! Finance, Fox News, the San Diego *Union Tribune*, Scottrade, MarketWire, and RealtyTrac, to name just a few media outlets.
Sam@investorinstitute.com
Mike@investorinstitute.com

Ronald P. Freeman is a Chicago-based mentor focused on helping people from all walks of life find freedom through real estate investing. Besides being a sought-after speaker, Ron has been featured in various publications and is considered a pioneer in his field. He has been investing in income producing properties since 1988 and has created a life of freedom that allows him to focus more on his philanthropy efforts. Email address: **ronaldpfreeman@yahoo.com**

Roxane Marie Schwabe is an intuitive facilitator, energy healer, spiritual teacher, and transformational speaker who conducts soul-nurturing exploration, inner light guidance, and training for self-healing, ceremonial blessing services, natural health seminars, and collaborative events with visionary and sound artists to celebrate higher consciousness.
RoxaneMarie@SimplyBeingSpirit.com

Roger Bishop is a human resources professional who has no equal at helping business owners make the workplace a positive environment while improving operations and employee performance. Life can be a positive, wonderful adventure when you apply daily, the lessons you learned growing up. He can be reached at **Roger@RogerCBishop.com**

Savannah Ross is the President of Rich Mom Enterprises Inc, an education based company dedicated to teaching a down to earth approach on creating great wealth through real estate investing. After a dramatic series of tragic events Savannah found herself on the brink of bankruptcy. Without any previous investment knowledge she then created over $3.1 Million in just 6 months. Just two years later, Savannah became the largest individual buyer of Real Estate in the Nation for 2009. Her system teaches a simple formula to acquiring high equity, high cash flow properties.

Savannah will be the first to tell you that she is not passionate about real estate or wealth. She has found them to be effective tools to allow her to follow her true passion of helping those less fortunate. By helping others create ultimate freedom, they too can follow their true purpose.

She is dedicated to empowering others to create their own success stories. Savannah and her family enjoy giving back by building homes and feeding families in third world countries. **www.richmom.com**

Shelley Radziminski is the owner and founder of Life Spirit Coaching. Working with high-level entrepreneurs, business owners, and the willing-able-and-ready in life, Shelley enables her clients to uncover their most powerful, heartfelt selves to create the lives of their dreams. With a strong background in science and a deep awareness of the greatness of the core spirit, Shelley has a unique ability to work with the intelligent to make them wiser and the compassionate to make them more productive. **www.LifeSpiritCoaching.com**

Steve Rodgers has been a proven leader in the real estate industry for nearly 20 years. He is president and owner/partner of a dominant San Diego real estate company. Steve was the president and CEO of Prudential California Realty, a division of Berkshire Hathaway affiliate Home Services America. He currently serves on several national and local realtor committees, and contributes year-round to schools, charities, community events, and many other worthy causes. Steve is married with two grown children and resides in San Diego. **steve@steverodgerstoday.com**

Tina Marie is the creator of the *Living to the Power of YES!,* a program course designed for individuals, corporations, and life coaches alike. Tina Marie Jones has brought together experience in business, entrepreneurism, adventurism, and family values and presents these fun and inspiring thoughts throughout the world. You can discover the *Power of YES!* for yourself at **www.tinamarie.com**

Valerie R. Sheppard is a recovering corporate executive on "radical sabbatical." She brings spiritual wisdom to her 28-plus years of experience in coaching to empower clients to be able to say, "I'm happy to be *me!*" She can be reached at:
www.valeriesheppard.com

Forthcoming projects
from Sherpa Press

- OFF THE COAST OF ZANZIBAR
  Summer 2011

Have a story to share?
Be featured in one of our best-selling titles.
Email **Allyn@SherpaPress.com** today, and learn how to
qualify to participate in an upcoming collaboration.

Visit us at: **www.SherpaPress.com**